A Necessary Life(Story)

Fiona Peacock

Dear Jillian

with best wishes

Dr fiona Peacock.

For the families and children I have worked with. I hope I gave to you just a fraction of the generosity and courage you shared with me. Each of you still has a place in my heart.

CONTENTS

Introduction

This is a book about Theraplay, specifically about Theraplay adapted for developmental and relational trauma. It isn't about the mechanics of games or working with the dimensions; there are manuals to help people with that. It is an exploration of the unseen, deep and hard-to-articulate work of Theraplay. Psychodynamically, I could call it working with the transference and countertransference phenomena. Or it could be termed 'working at relational depth'. Or finding the motivation of the client to change.

I would suggest that whatever your core approach to therapeutic help, at the heart of it is the struggle to create a meaningful relationship. This work of fiction seeks to illuminate that process in Theraplay practice with people for whom relationship itself is the source of distress.

The approach I chose to take in a doctoral research process was using heuristic inquiry to illuminate the tacit knowledge I use in my Theraplay practice with children who are Looked After or Adopted in the UK. Sandy Sela-Smith (2002) describes tacit knowledge as "that internal place where experience, feeling and meaning go together to form both a picture of the world and a way to navigate that world". She calls this the "final frontier" of exploration of our inner experiences, where feeling is the dominant component of understanding and making meaning of our worlds. This story, in this form, is the "findings" of my research as well as the "process" of illuminating that knowledge. As Sela-Smith said, engaging with this final frontier means putting aside certainty and leaping into the subjective unknown on the parts of both the writer and the reader. There may be another version of this story in the future adapted to be a training tool for Theraplay practitioners.

The most dangerous stories are those that have never been given words. They are the stories that say *I must not get up before the man or go to bed after the man*. They are the stories that say *I must be afraid of the man and that who I am depends on how the man sees me*. They are the stories that say that *the man is the most powerful and smartest and wisest, so my strength and insights and fortitude are fallacious and affects and nonsenses*. They are the stories that say *my slowness is bad, my worry is bad, my care is bad, my sense of humour is bad, my carefreeness is bad, my creativity is bad*. They are the stories that say *I am bad*. And they are the stories I have been living by.

The stories of Milo and Joe may be made of a different fabric and tone and colour and hue to the stories of our clients, or indeed ourselves, but the way they are embodied may be the same. This is a story that tries to put into words the unspoken stories that bind and blind, in the hope of freedom, peace and wisdom.

———————————

Sela-Smith (2002) Heuristic Research: A Review and Critique of Moustakas's Method *Journal of Humanistic Psychology*, 42(3), 53-88

CHAPTER ONE

Birth Stories

Joe is born.

It was a moment. For just that moment everything stopped: sound, speed, confusions.

And then there was light.

She had done it.

The baby was hers, here.

Him.

She hadn't been that sure there was a baby. She hadn't been sure if it was a baby that it would be OK. It – he – had been injured into her, or loved into her, by someone, by its/his father. Who? Dark confusions.

And then she saw him. He was given to her. The noise, the rush, the muddle started all over again.

In that still moment, he had named himself.

Emmanuel.

He would never be called that except in her heart. In that one still moment, he had filled her whole heart.

Held in light, silence and stillness.

He opened his eyes, closed them, turned his head and pushed it into her. For that moment he, too, knew in his flesh that he had filled her whole heart.

Val is born.

The last two months had been hard. Pre-eclampsia had stolen her plans and her self-control. The home birth had been taken from her, and the delivery forced by invasion and fear.

And it was a girl.

Not at any time in the 34 weeks had she ever thought it was going to be a girl. What would she do with one of those?

She only saw it briefly before they took it to check it, swooping it away to the special care baby unit. She felt battered and drawn out. They asked if she would like to be wheeled through to see her daughter, and she said no.

It had been a struggle to keep that spark glowing while she carried the child; now the child was out in the open, the spark was extinguished. The infant was small. They thought it would survive but there was some risk. Frightened of that feeling, she blinked and stared at the infant.

Later, she expressed milk and they fed the child with a tube. The child would be taken home and all the right things would be said and done, but there would be empty stillness and hurtful silence.

Grace is born.

The midwife had been blunt. "Your fourth? You're an experienced mother. You don't need to be here for long." She was pleased to be going home so soon. Three boys and now their daughter. She couldn't keep the smile away from her face. She knew as soon as she got through the door that the boys would launch at her with books and Lego and arguments, and she would love every moment of it. Her daughter would tune in and become part of the band.

Once home, her husband steered her to the bedroom, seeing her weariness. She was exhausted. Their daughter latched on, and milk and love flowed between them. Then sleep.

Even then, the smile couldn't leave her. Her partner looked at her and thought they were the most beautiful sight ever seen.

Milo is born

No one was certain if his mother even knew she was pregnant. She'd already had three children removed and adopted. She didn't attend any antenatal check-ups. She had a history of drinking and suspected drug use. The boy was born onto a filthy bathroom floor. The paramedics who arrived found the house in a disgusting state – dog faeces on the lounge floor, plates left out, looking clean, except the paramedic then saw one of the family dogs nosing into a pizza box and suspected they had licked the plates clean.

In hospital, his mother showed no interest in the infant. The midwife set in motion an assessment. His mother did enough to get people off her back so she could get out of the place, taking the baby with her.

It was Christmas time when the police were called to the house because of reports of a domestic. They found a Christmas tree strewn over the floor, a woman bleeding with a black eye, a man passed out, drunk, and a young child curled up with the dogs seemingly asleep. They took him to a place of safety.

CHAPTER TWO

An Unexpected Email

Are you Val, the therapist who used to work for social services in 2006? If you are, I just wanted to tell you that I am going to be a dad and to say thank you. You might not remember me. Joe.

Val looked at the email, astonished. There were some cases that always stick with you; Joe had been one of those. She had always wondered if she had done anything of any use for him.

What should she do? What were the ethics of a newly retired therapist being contacted by an ex-client who would now be, what, 19 years old? She guessed he'd still be somewhat vulnerable. His life had been a big muddle when she was seeing him. Surely it could be detrimental not to respond? What would Brenda have said?

She missed her supervisor. Her death had been one of the things that had propelled her into the final choice to retire. The thought of establishing a relationship with a new supervisor felt "tiring", so she knew that was the point to end her direct work with children. She still supervised others in their Theraplay practice; it gave her great pleasure, especially seeing trainees develop from novices in the method to becoming fully fledged, experienced practitioners.

What would she say to one of her supervisees? A novice, she might say go back to social services. To someone experienced, she would explore things more. She could almost see Brenda smile at her. "You're a grown-up, Val, think it through yourself."

The trouble with children like Joe was that her head had been so tangled by the case, and the time of her life, that it had been hard to know which were the children's stuff and which were her own. But why should that deprive Joe of what she could offer him now? Not to respond would be far more about her insecurity than professional ethics. The "rules" might direct her to tell him to go to social services, but how did that live out the ethic of caring? How did that honour the commitment she still held to the relationship? She was sure she wasn't being reckless with her ethical responsibility when she responded.

Hi Joe, she emailed back. *I remember you well. You are going to be a father? Wow! Is that something you would like to talk to someone about? Kind regards, Val.*

They did meet, in a coffee shop. He was still pretty short and wired. His eyes still danced in the way she remembered. His social worker had described him like a kitten who felt such excitement that he'd lose control of his muscles and would fall over. Maybe that energy was a little less all over the place and he had found some harmony with it. She bought herself a tea, and he said he wanted a coke. As they sat, he told her about his life after they had finished working together.

He'd stayed with Nickie his foster carer until he was 14 and then she couldn't care for him anymore. "I was doing drugs," he said. "I wasn't listening to her." They still stayed in touch. She still loved him. It was just that she couldn't keep him safe anymore. Joe was open and so totally sure of her love for him. He didn't dress up events for Val. When Nickie tried to keep him safe, Joe pushed her, hit her and gave her a black eye.

So that was that.

"She did the right thing," Joe said, "getting them to move me. I could have hurt her."

He bounced from emergency placement to residential then, when he pulled a knife on a teacher at school, to a secure placement. In secure, they carried out a psychology assessment, and found his working memory to be poor and his dyslexia so severe that his capacity to read and retain information in words was a significant handicap. But they taught him to decorate and paint, and he started to find pleasure in making things beautiful. He told it all to Val in such a matter-of-fact tone that the enormity of what he was saying went over her head.

He was set up in a flat by himself when he was 17 and would take in people who were less OK than he was. He couldn't bear to see people younger than he was sleeping rough. One of those was a girl. She went by the name of Shell.

Michelle? Val wondered.

She was the person who was going to have his baby and make him a dad. He fair swelled with pride at the thought of being a dad.

"I want to be a good one," he said, and then he looked really serious. "Val, I don't want to be a dad like my dad was to me and my mum. I'm not going to be like that, am I?"

Val longed to reach out and touch his hand. She could just see the little boy she was unable to catch in school when he was six. "The devil himself" one teacher had called him, but it was said with a smile. Joe somehow had always been able to do that – get people to love him despite his language and behaviour.

"Joe, you want to be a good dad, and you can be. Can you let people help you to do that?"

"Yeah," Joe said. "Nickie has said she'll help me and Shell. She was good to me; she never let me down. Even when I hurt her, she still came to see me. I said she was going to be Granny."

"What do you remember about the work we did together?" Val was curious.

"I just remember you and Mum playing with me. They were weird games. I never did understand what you were on about. But, yeah, I suppose I think I could do some of the same stuff with my baby when she is born."

"You don't remember it being just you and me?"

"No. Did that happen? I only remember it being you and Mum."

"Joe." Val's voice was low and tentative, not wanting to put him in a difficult position but feeling she had such a unique chance to understand the process of Theraplay for a child. "I'm retired now, but I'm doing some research. I really want to know what the Theraplay was like for people. If I talked to you more about that time, would you let me use it for my research?"

"Yeah, of course." Joe didn't hesitate.

Was she using him? Did she need to protect him from himself? Brenda's voice came in again: "You are a grown-up. Strong, wise and kind."

Transcription of research interview and field notes.
Transcribed by Val Ingrams. Added notes by Val Ingrams.

The interview took place in a fairly large room at a children's centre with toys all around. It was the only venue I could get near to where Joe was living, and I also thought it might be a first step in putting him in touch with a service that he, his partner and their baby may benefit from.

Val: Joe, thank you for meeting with me.

Joe looked a strange combination of shifty and laid back. He was dressed in jeans and a T-shirt, his legs thrust out towards her as he leant back in the chair as if to say "look at my trainers". I wondered if the trainers were significant, but I didn't want to show my ignorance of what was on trend at the moment. Although he looked as if he was relaxed, his body was angled awkwardly and his fingers kept going to his mouth. He gave me a quick glance, a fleeting moment of eye contact, as if to confirm my greeting to him.

Val: So, how old are you now?

Joe: 19.

Val: That makes it 13 years since I last saw you?

Joe: I dunno.

Val: What have you been doing since I last saw you when you were 6?

Joe sat up a little more – was that more tension or a sign that he was interested?

Joe: I had to leave Nickie when I was 14. They put me in a children's home.

Val: How come you left Nickie's?

Joe's face dropped for a moment before that "I'm OK" persona came back. He locked his gaze onto Val and then just as quickly dropped it as if, without being aware, he was gauging what he could allow himself to say.

Joe: I was bad. I got big and I scared her.

Val: Did you stay in touch.

Joe looked really surprised.

Joe: Of course. I went there every Sunday to have dinner. She's looking forward to being a granny.

Val: Then what happened, after you went to the children's home.

Joe: It was a laugh. You didn't have to go to school or anything. When I did go to school, we messed around; and I once got pissed off and pulled a knife on a teacher and got sent to secure. They showed me how to do painting and decorating, but I can't get a job coz I've got that crime. Then when you were 17, they made you go and live in a flat on your own. Nickie showed me how to clean. It was all right. I was doing art at college, but it was hard to get up on time.

Val: So what do you feel about the teacher and the knife now?

Joe: Yeah, I didn't mean to hurt him, but he shouldn't have pissed me off. Secure was all right. Kids' prison. I got my GCSE Maths and English, and they taught me stuff about living on my own.

Val: So, what do you do now?

Joe: Play games, see Shell, get ready for our baby.

Val: Do you have a job at all?

Joe: Nah, who'd have me? Besides, I don't want to be tied down to what other people want of me.

Val: Do you remember our work together?

Joe: I remember playing; we did really silly games. You didn't make me talk about anything.

Val: And not making you talk about anything, was that good or not good?

Joe paused. I had the distinct impression that there were two Joes in front of me: the Joe who had to be full of bravado and don't-careishness, fulfilling the expectations of the "wastrel and feckless youth, ill-equipped by the care system to be a productive member of society" and the Joe I had seen as a child, quick-witted, funny, sharply insightful, and as loving as he could be. It was as if they were battling it out. Who could he be? I felt tears prick in my eyes. Why? Was this the painful battle that Joe had to balance day by day?

Hearing Joe talk about going to Sunday dinner with Nickie had seemed so normal. Now it was painful to see him in this state of dilemma, but I remembered, this isn't therapy, this is an interview. I didn't want him to stay in that state for long – it wasn't fair. I got the bubble mix out of my bag and blew bubbles.

Joe: God, I remember you doing that! I had forgotten till you did it. I sat on Nickie's lap and you blew bubbles.

Joe's face broke into a huge smile and there was a softening of his posture. He reached up one finger to a bubble that was drifting towards him.

Joe: We used to pop them; you would tell me which finger to use and I would do it. God, I really never did what I was told then, did I? I was a little sod.

Val: Tell me about Shell.

Joe: She is 16. She's just left care, went to the same children's home I was in. You should see her arms; they are cut from here to here.

Joe pointed from his wrists to the top of his arms.

Joe: We are going to make a better life for our baby. I'll blow bubbles for her.

Val: Do you know it is going to be a girl?

Joe: Nah, I just hope it is so I can look after her properly. Me and Shell, we are going to try and get a place together when the baby is born.

I found myself thinking about the way in which Joe had battered and rejected the dolls in the work we did together, the times when I had tried to give him a sense of how an infant may be cared for. I tried to adapt the Theraplay to try to help him when direct nurture was just too raw, too much for him. He had screamed with such a pitch when I played peek-a-boo with the baby doll's feet. I thought it had really triggered a trauma memory.

Joe: What happened to me, Val?

For just a moment Joe was 19, a young man, grown up, hurting, wanting to live a life of care and love with his new family but knowing there was something unimaginably dreadful in his early life.

Val: Joe, we never knew. There was stuff we wondered about, but your mum and dad never said. I don't even know if they knew that what they were doing might not be right for a child. I think you saw stuff no child should ever see and stuff was done to you that should never be done to a child and you survived as best you could. Joe, promise me, when your baby is born, find someone to talk to. Your baby might bring back feelings of what it was like when you were little. Not just for you but for Shell as well. I can hear that you want to give your child a different life, but to do that you have to let go of the life you had to bear when you were little.

I felt agitated and I could also see that I had lost Joe.

Where would he have been without the Theraplay? Who knows? Maybe the shove to Nickie would have been with a knife. Maybe the knife to the teacher wouldn't have been "messing around" but something bigger and more aggressive. Maybe his girlfriend would have been the victim of a rape or their relationship would have been marked by domestic violence. Without the labour that Nickie, Joe's social worker and his school had put in, and the Theraplay we did together, maybe Joe wouldn't have been able to know that he wanted to give his child a different start in life to the one he had. Maybe the wheel was turning for Joe's child in a better, less traumatic way. I wished I could see the whole story, but I couldn't. I had to find within myself the ability to be content with what I had done.

CHAPTER THREE

A Music Barely Heard

"..., or music heard so deeply
That it is not heard at all, but you are the music
While the music lasts. These are only hints and guesses,
Hints, followed by guesses; and the rest
Is prayer, observance, discipline, thought and action.
The hint half guessed, the gift half understood, is
Incarnation."

T. S. Eliot, 'The Dry Salvages' (Eliot. 1974. *Collected Poems: 1909–1962)* Faber and Faber

Val sighed. Car parking at County Hall was such a nightmare. She had already driven around the car park twice hoping that someone would leave and make it possible for her to park.

One more time, she thought to herself, *and then I will leave.*

She sighed again, angry at herself – if only she had left more time, if only she had decided to park in the multi-story, if only... And now if she had to park on the other side of the town, she would be late for the meeting, but what could she do?

It had taken weeks to find a time when everyone could be in the same room at the same time: the adoption social worker and her manager; the parents; the child's social worker. Val had asked for the child's school to send someone as well, but that had just been too difficult. In the end, given that the placement sounded like it was about to disrupt, Val decided they just had to go ahead. She hadn't even been able to get everyone to come to her consulting room; hence, she ended up with the headache of parking at County Hall.

She was so lost in her thoughts that she almost missed the space. She reversed quickly before someone else came along – yes, it was against the rules, but if she drove all around the car park again, someone else would have got there first. A horn sounded and lights flashed at her; she went into County Hall trying to keep a lid on a sense of guilt by telling herself that the ends justified the means for a little boy who was waiting for help, and pretending not to notice the anger she felt about having to organise such a meeting when she was the therapist not a social worker.

The meeting "went well".

"Flat" was the word that came to Val's mind. Such a familiar story. He'd been neglected. Removed from his family at Christmas time after a domestic incident. The infestation of head lice was so severe that his head was sore and weeping. He was nearing the age of five but hadn't been registered for school. Social Care had been in and out of the family all of his life, but, until the incident at Christmas, they had co-operated just enough so that Social Care couldn't quite make the decision to take him into care. Post removal, when he was hospitalised because of infection due to head lice, they found old injuries. His parents didn't go to visit him, and almost by default he went to a foster carer and a year later to Melanie and Simon who had been waiting to adopt for 18 months. It had been messy.

Milo's social worker, Louise, wouldn't say it to their face, but she thought Mel and Simon didn't show enough affection to Milo. She thought that if only they were warmer, he would have settled by now. She thought that if they were less caught up in their smart house and demanding careers, then it would be fine; although, this was more of a feeling lodged just beneath her conscious thought. That she and her partner had to live with her partner's parents because, despite their joint wages as caring professionals, they couldn't even afford to rent was "just life". To her, Mel's protestations that something was wrong with Milo were vague, petty, maybe a sign that Mel was emotionally unavailable. She had questioned the assessing social worker in private about Mel's mental health history. Had that been adequately assessed when Mel and Simon were approved as adopters? In her busy repertoire of professional cognisance, she had no space for the unthinkable thought of envy.

Val had felt that she was trying to make a jigsaw puzzle out of an indeterminate and constantly changing number of pieces. She didn't even have a picture to help her start. All of those fragmented phone calls and emails and long answerphone messages were part of the meeting but weren't spoken about. Mel trying to find the words to say what she felt was wrong: bed-wetting; not doing as he was told; finding empty – and full – crisp packets stuffed down the back of the wardrobe; and telling lies. No one else seeing all of this, as if he saved it up to make them suffer at home. Was he mad? What could he be diagnosed with? Just make him better.

Somehow, the most important information was still left unsaid.

So, she could say she was using the Theraplay protocol she had needed to hold the meeting, but Val knew what her response would be from the start. It was what she did with all of these cases.

"I think I have something that will help. It is called Theraplay, and we start with a MIM – that's a Marschak Interaction Method. Mel, I will meet with you and Milo and give you different activities to do. I will video you doing them so I can see what works well between you and what things I can help the pair of you do better."

The sigh of relief in the room was palpable, if not audible. Someone was going to "do something". Everyone left chatting.

"Flat" was the word that kept weighing on Val's mind.

It still took a hell of a long time to set up the MIM.

The school secretary: "Play therapy? Oh no, the last one left the room in a terrible mess."

Val just didn't have the energy to explain yet again that Theraplay wasn't the same as play therapy. Uncharitably, she wished she could wring the "play therapist's" neck.

The head teacher, Mr Brewer: "But why do you want to do it in school? We don't have any problems with Milo."

Val had to offer lots of patient explanation, lots of soothing and nurture, and lots of creation of structure before a small room could be made available.

"It is a very busy time of the year and our space is very limited, but you could use room B12. I'm afraid at the moment we're storing our spare tables in there while the storeroom is decorated."

At least, Val thought, *we weren't put in the storeroom itself.* And again, she caught herself and tried to metaphorically look herself in the eye. Where was this lack of unconditional positive regard coming from? This world weariness?

14

Milo's social worker, impatiently: "Do you have a date yet? The guardian ad litem is really concerned about this placement. Your report will help a lot in deciding if Milo should stay there."

Val exhaled rapidly, holding the phone away from her in the hope that the social worker wouldn't hear it. She settled herself into her seat, making sure she was aware of the contact points, making sure she filled her lungs fully again and spoke from deep within herself. Thank goodness for her yoga class.

"Remember, Louise, this work is being commissioned by the adoption team, and the purpose of the assessment is to see how I can help Milo, Simon and Mel move forwards. It would be a different focus if I were being asked to assess the viability of the placement. What comes out may be helpful to you, but that isn't what I have been asked to do."

Louise didn't have the awareness to hold the phone away from herself. Val heard the "harrumph" of Louise's breath and the tightness in her voice: "We are all trying to make sure Milo has the best chance."

The call ended with this tension and Val felt her body sag. She felt like a sponge sucking in the negativity and at the same time vaguely enjoyed the challenge of being the puzzle master of all these pieces. She quite deliberately chose to go into her head, to stay with the intellectual challenge of the puzzle. What part of the picture needed to be in place next? Had she made any clarity in any part of the frame? It comforted her, this going to the headspace. It felt a bit more as though she had some control over the process, but she also felt a weight, something a bit out of her focus, a vague blur that dissipated when she tried to turn to look at it.

She massaged her eyebrows and the back of her neck, but the tension was still out of her reach. If she tried to focus, she found tears coming to her eyes. *But that's not Milo*, she thought. *How could it be?* She hadn't even met him yet. *I think that's me.* Even finally having a date for the MIM didn't take away that disconnect, that "I-don't-know-what-this-is-about" feeling, that glum flatness that filled all of her.

Clench one buttock, then the other. Push the back to the left. Aah, good feel. Stretch. Ears everywhere. Eyes forward. Eyes wide. Pull toes up. Aah, stretch. Good feel. Movement. Where? Emma!

Milo's hand was the first to shoot up, so fast that Miss Honey was sure that his bottom must have risen at least 10 centimetres off his seat. He was always first, but she asked Emma on the back row who was just a fraction slower.

For a moment, Milo felt really present. The rapid energy of putting up his hand like that meant for a while he felt alert and calm, his thoughts settled on what was happening now, for a moment. Numeracy, always the first lesson of the day. Mum had said a nice lady was coming to see him in school today. He hoped it wasn't a social worker.

Body starts to sink. Ugh, stretch in shoulders. Stomach. Lungs. Compress. Throat close. The feeling is really deep. Unstabilising. Pee about to come. Vestigial awareness. Slight movement somewhere. Do.

This time the hand shot up with such vigour that Milo was on his feet. Miss Honey smiled. He was so enthusiastic, not that he ever got the questions right.

"Milo?" she invited.

"Umm…"

Numeracy, first lesson. More here? Not going to pee now, don't know, aware of eyes. Think of a number.

"…five."

"No, Milo." Everyone else could hear the smile in Miss Honey's voice. She exchanged a glance with Mrs Dramowicz, her classroom assistant. They both liked Milo. "Good try, though. Who else?"

Milo sank into the chair grinding his teeth.

A nice lady? What? Need. Bite. Pencil. Looks like working. Can't do too much. Pencil on paper. Sound. Chew sleeve. Need!

Rav, two rows back, was fidgeting. Miss Honey started to walk towards him. *Loser*, thought Milo. I can do it and no one knows.

"Miss," someone called from across the class.

Miss Honey turned as she said, "I'll come to you after I've seen Rav." And in that moment, Milo threw his pencil at Rav.

Full turn one way. Full turn the other. Pull. Hurl. Crash knees on underside of desk. Elbow into girl next to me. She won't tell. Pathetic. Wimp. Grab her pencil.

"Miss!" Rav whined. "Milo just threw his pencil at me!"

Miss Honey looked perplexed. "But Milo is writing with his pencil." She squatted down next to Rav. "If you are finding it hard, Rav, just ask. Now, the way we do this is…"

The building-up was happening again. Out of control. Right buttock. Left buttock. Side stretch. One way. Other way. Bite sleeve. Bite pencil. Everyone still. Ears everywhere. Where with eyes? Look at work – but what is happening?

Door opens.

Mum.

Milo hurled himself across the classroom and buried his head into Mel's stomach. She was taken by surprise. She hadn't known Milo to greet her like that before. She had to take two steps back to balance herself. Like a cannon ball, she felt that he was going to go right through her and out the other side. It felt like everyone must be able to see all of her innards and she had to just carry on.

"Is it OK to take Milo now, Miss Honey?" she asked.

"Of course."

Miss Honey thought it was wonderful the way Milo loved his mum. You could just see it from the way he greeted her. Such a lovely boy with such a rough start. She sighed. Aware of...? Something niggled inside her... Feeling a bit more...? More? But then other children were asking her how to complete the task, so she moved on.

Mr Brewer was walking past the class. That Miss Honey, she was a star. She was very young, just a newly qualified teacher, but he had seen it when he interviewed her. She could just get a class to "flow". It was beautiful to see – all those children working together but at their own pace. They all looked so relaxed, like they were steady and comfortable in each other's presence. She had such a talent. He was looking forward to seeing that talent blossom.

When the classroom was cleaned that night, the cleaner found a chewed pencil under the radiator. She put it in the bin. *Poor kid*, she thought. *He'd had a hard day.*

Val sat there waiting. She had done everything she could – covering the spare tables with a sheet, setting out a corner, making it comfortable with cushions, putting out the box with the 10 MIM instructions and all the things Mel and Milo might need. She checked and rechecked the camera – battery OK, enough memory on the card, focused on the right spot. Of course they were all OK. She had done this often enough – and messed up the camera often enough – to have done all that checking before she even arrived. It made her aware of just how anxious she was about meeting a child for the first time, having all those half-portraits of him from different people but not really knowing him at all.

The door opened and Mel came in. From all she had heard about Milo, Val wasn't sure whether to expect the child to bounce in or creep in. In real life, he just held his mother's hand.

"Hello," Val said, almost shyly. "I'm Val." He gave her a look and, fleetingly, she had an odd flash of panic that passed so rapidly that she wasn't sure it had happened at all. The whole experience left her feeling a bit off balance.

The structure of the MIM came to her rescue.

"You and Mum make yourselves comfortable on the cushions, and I will tell you what we are doing today."

That look again. For a moment, even though she had made her voice as strong and directive as possible, she thought he was going to say, "No." Not yet.

He let Mel take him across the room and they settled on the cushions. Val sat on the floor opposite them and smiled – mostly for Mel's benefit. Mel smiled back. Milo squirmed into his mother as if seeking comfort, but his eyes were still on Val.

How, thought Val, *can a child look so moulded to his mother but still look so separate?* Out loud she said, "Did Mum tell you about today?"

"No," Milo said. But Val knew that Mel had because they'd talked about what she should say to him.

"Well, I have the best job in the world. I go around and play with families and see how I can help them have even better times together. Today, I am going to get you and Mum to do some things together so I can see what you do well and how I can help you have even more fun."

He's not buying this, Val was thinking. She could feel the slight stiffening of her throat and chest in response to the slight stiffening of his body. He was sitting straighter now, less glued to Mel. It could have been that he was settling and didn't need comfort anymore – except that she hadn't seen him getting any comfort. It was more, she thought, like when her cat was wondering whether it was worth stalking a bird or not. Not in full fight mode, but at that point where it looked as if he was thinking, *I can if I need to. Or want to. Or just for the hell of it because that's what a cat does.* She noted the thought and noted the sensation in the pit of her stomach.

"What you do is take each of the envelopes from the box. They are all numbered. You do the activity in the envelope. You can take as long or as little time as you like. There is absolutely no right or wrong way of doing these activities, and if there are any you read and think nah, don't want to do that, that's fine, just go on to the next one. Any questions? OK, I'll turn the camera on…and whenever you're ready, you can start."

Milo immediately reached for the first envelope, and Mel let him take it. He started to read the card but struggled with the words, so Mel stepped in to help him spell it out. *Like a teacher*, Val thought.

Afterwards, she was ashamed to admit that her attention wandered during the first few activities. It all seemed so predictable to her. Milo seeking control so subtly; Mel falling for it each time. Mel going up into her head too much, being a teacher, trying to wrest any sort of control back again. And then suddenly Val felt her attention snap back. Even looking at the video of the session later, she still couldn't work out what it was that grabbed her by the head and heart and guts at that moment.

It was the task about drawing. The instructions were "Adult and child each take paper and pencil. Adult draws quick picture, encourages child to copy".

Brenda had been aware for a little while that Val was starting to "wear out". As someone she had supervised for a long time, initially she hadn't seen the subtle signs; and she felt a degree of guilt about not seeing Val's distress sooner. It had just become so much more apparent in the last couple of months where, frankly, clinical supervision had become boring. Val would come, present the case, talk about difficulties and just want a "what to do next" answer. When they had started working together, Val would really "chew over" what was going on in the room, in the moment, in herself, in the child and family she was engaged with.

So, it was a huge relief to Brenda when Val came in looking agitated and said, "I don't know what to do."

After Val had given a short précis of the background, it seemed time, to Brenda, to see if they could unpick what was really going on.

"Put it in a sentence," she said, "what do you really want from supervision?"

It didn't take Val long. In fact, she had been thinking about this so much since the MIM, since looking at the video on her own and being unable to make sense of why, during the assessment, she was suddenly electrified. "What happened?" was all she said.

"Play me the video. Find me a spot where you feel it again, and stop the tape."

Val did.

"Now really look at that image and tell me what you see?"

"It's the drawing task. Mel's body is open but at the same time she is defensive – like she is open but at the same time putting a barrier between her and Milo. She is helping Milo. She was good at breaking the task down into manageable bits, and she made it interesting to him. She drew something she knew he would like."

"Stick with the image. What do you see?"

"Milo's face has relaxed." Val felt tears come to her eyes as she said this. *Bizarre*, she thought.

"He's put his head on his mum's arm. He's looking at the picture they are drawing together. It's not all OK. His legs are pushed into his mum, but his mouth... He's not smiling...but it's normal."

Val paused trying to hear the meaning of her own words. It was too hard; it was like...it was...like... The image that came to Val was that of a current under the water at the bend of the river: idyllic but deadly. The trust she had in Brenda from their long time working together meant that she didn't have to edit the thought or ignore it. She could just say it even if it seemed initially meaningless.

"Hold on to that," was all Brenda said. "Is there another moment in the video that 'gets you'?"

Val let the video run again. She stopped it at the moment her stomach dropped. "It's here," she said. She didn't need Brenda's prompt this time. "It's the lotion activity. Mel had lotioned Milo's arms, and he really didn't like it, but then it was his turn to lotion her. He couldn't get the lid off the bottle, so she helped him. She broke it down into little steps and showed him how, and then let him do it himself so he was successful. He was so unsure about the lotion; his fingers were all tense and his tongue was sticking out. He looks his age, maybe younger. He used just one finger and put it on her arm, and for a moment he looks into Mel's eyes – that's where I have stopped it. It looks like Mel is melting. It's so fleeting." Not tears this time. Val felt like her jaw was dropping. Her head felt weighed down too. She looked at Brenda and was aware that she hadn't made eye contact with her supervisor for many sessions.

Brenda saw that, too. "If Milo could speak at that moment, what do you think he would say?"

"I want to love you, but I'm too scared?"

Brenda held the eye contact, and Val allowed herself to be seen.

"What's really going on, Val?" Brenda asked.

"They are trying so hard, both of them and..."

"Not to them, you!" Brenda had to work to keep Val's eyes in that moment. Briefly, she thought she had pushed too hard, too soon, but then it came. Slowly first and then as sobs. Inwardly, Brenda smiled. Now she knew Val would be OK.

The parent feedback session took place at the family home. When Val had phoned Mel to arrange the time, Mel had come up with many reasons why she couldn't come to the office: Simon was away on business; her mum was poorly so she needed to be available for her. After her supervision with Brenda, it was easy for Val to allow the notion of "excuses" to dissolve and hear that Mel was having a tough time and needed the containing safety of her own home.

It was a beautiful home, well-tended with large, airy rooms. Mel looked strangely small and huddled on the sofa in the sitting room. The family's large black Labrador, Sophie, settled calmly in her basket once her exuberant and affectionate greeting of Val was over.

"How do you feel the MIM went?" Val asked.

Mel shook her head slowly and sighed. "I just don't know what I am doing. It feels like he is out to get me."

Val felt her heart go out to Mel, especially having watched the video of the MIM many times since her supervision. "Let's have a look at what I saw."

The first section Val played was the "drawing" activity, the one that had caught her attention in supervision. She had reflected and viewed it and thought about it over and over again. It *had* triggered some of her own sense of loss and despair. She was also pretty sure that that part of her personal experience had been touched because it was there for Milo too. He had kind of told her, so quietly without any words. She stopped the clip at the same place she had in supervision.

Mel was sitting straighter on the sofa, her gaze a bit more focused.

"What did you see?" Val asked.

"I'm not sure," Mel replied. "I just noticed how much I kept touching him and how much I kept interfering in what he was drawing. Maybe I should leave him alone to get on with things more."

Val rewound the video by just a couple of seconds. "Look at his face here," she said. "What do you see now?"

"He's smiling?"

"Why not make that expression with your own face?"

Gamely, Mel did. Val felt herself doing the same, feeling the stretch around her mouth and lips and the tautness around her eyes.

"That's not a smile, is it?" Mel said.

"I don't think it is. When I saw it and thought about it, it seemed more of a grimace, or a way of keeping us out. It's a defence, I think, and it distracts us as it kind of looks like a smile."

Mel was on the edge of the seat now. "And his eyes! It's like he's not there and he's scared too! I feel scared when I make my eyes like that!"

"Now look at this one again." Val stopped the video in the same place as before. "What do you see in his face now?" This time she could see that Mel didn't need the prompt to make her body into the same shape as Milo's, nor to let her face copy the expression on his.

"Oh," she said.

"Yes." Val let Mel reflect on the image for a while and then said, "You do such a good job of giving him structure in this activity that for a moment he can relax. But what do you think about your body language?"

Mel contemplated the image. "He can't get inside me, can he?"

Val knew she was referring to the way she held her arms and legs, and she felt that Mel had worded it in such an insightful way. "Let's have a look at this one next..." She showed Mel the lotion activity. "Remember the instruction was 'Adult and child each take one bottle of lotion, apply lotion to each other'." She allowed the video to play without pausing.

Sophie came over and put her head on Mel's lap. Mel absent-mindedly fondled Sophie's ears as she watched.

"We got Sophie when I found out I couldn't have children," Mel said.

Val did her best not to display her surprise at this seeming change in direction. Sometimes these things go in directions you don't expect.

"She was the boldest in the litter; she was the one who crawled out of the basket and came over to us." The smile spread across Mel's face before the words came out. "She wagged her tail so hard her body couldn't take it and she fell over. But when we brought her home, she really seemed to miss her litter. She just kept crying, and there was nothing I could do. In the end, Simon undid his shirt and put her next to his skin and she just fell asleep there." Mel made fierce eye contact. "I hated him for that; I was so jealous. Sophie has been his dog ever since. I did all the puppy training and clearing up the messes and the trips to the vets, and he'd walk in the door and she'd be in ecstasy." Mel was silent for a moment. She was still gently stroking Sophie's ears. There were tears flowing quietly down her face. Sophie's head was on her lap, still, her eyes on Mel's face, Mel looking at her.

Val waited, not wanting to rush the moment. In the end, she needed to ask, "Why do you think that memory came to mind when you looked at this picture of you and Milo?"

It almost looked as if Mel was moving underwater or coming back from a dream to look at the video still on the laptop. The words seemed to come from a long way down: "We both want...we both want to love. But I want my baby. I can't let him in because he isn't the baby I want."

Val also felt lost in the moment, not really consciously forming her responses but going with her internal flow. "And you aren't the mummy he wants either. He wants his mummy."

"But we can't have them can we. I can't have a baby and his mummy hurt him." Now Sophie almost seemed to want to get onto Mel's lap.

Val looked at the image on the screen again. "And here it looks like you both want to give each other nurture but something gets in the way." Immediately, she wished those words hadn't come out of her mouth – they just didn't do justice to the feeling of the moment.

She looked back at Mel. Something was processing. Sophie was right up now, and Mel barely noticed herself putting her arms around the dog. The dog then curled up on her lap, awkward and really too weighty. Val just kept watching. Mel's breathing became deeper, moving from the top of her lungs, downwards, until there was a sense of peace about her. She hefted Sophie to one side without pushing her off her lap entirely. Sophie grumbled but accepted it. Mel reached for her bag and pulled out her phone. It was another switch in direction that took Val by surprise.

"We went away last weekend. To some a castle. Milo was such a pain. We couldn't really look round at all. Then we found this children's playground." She was fiddling with the phone as she spoke. "He ran around like a mad thing and then got on one of those, you know, huge basket swings that they've put in lots of playgrounds now. The ones that are big enough to get loads of children in. I think he was so tired; he just lay there. Simon joined him and held him, and I pushed the swing. I took pictures, and then Simon took pictures of me and Milo. Then a lady came by and asked if we would like a picture of all of us. I think I must have looked a bit suspicious because she said she remembered how hard it was to get a picture of all of them together when hers were little. She took this."

Mel held out the phone. The three of them. Milo between them on the swing. All smiling. Simon looking at Mel. Milo holding onto Mel.

"We look like a family," Mel said. "When I wonder if we can go on, I look at it and think we are a family. Is it my fault? Is it me that's stopping him loving us?"

"No. You're hurt because you've lost your chance for your own baby. He's hurt because he's lost his mummy. Somehow you just find the ways to love each other, despite the hurt; and finding that makes the hurt less painful, but I don't think it ever really all goes away."

"So how do I start?" Mel asked.

CHAPTER FOUR

Beginnings

The other new referral was more what Val expected. A placement social worker had contacted a child care social worker to say that her foster carer was struggling with a young boy who'd been in placement for four months. Several previous placements had broken down and unless the child received therapy, this one would break down as well. She'd been to CAMHS (Child and Adolescent Mental Health Services) and they'd said that as it wasn't a permanent placement, they wouldn't see the child. They added that as it was behavioural, not a mental health problem, even if the placement had been permanent, they wouldn't have seen him. When the childcare social worker rang Val to see if she could offer something, the story came out in a breathless way. Val made arrangements for that social worker, Grace, to come to The Cottage to meet her.

Val had held a dream about The Cottage long before it became a reality. She wanted a place in the countryside that could be set up like a home where families could come for their therapy. There was a kitchen where they could cook together if that's what was needed. There was a lounge for parents to relax while their child had individual therapy and a special Theraplay room. The floor was soft, no furniture but cushions and a one-way mirror with a viewing room and cameras that could be controlled remotely so action could be followed around the room. There were two more general therapy rooms, one big enough for groups. In all the rooms, therapy could be captured on video.

The three therapists had clubbed together to set up The Cottage Therapy Centre. Two had lost their parents and gained a legacy, and one had a husband with a job that paid well. It had been enough of a deposit to secure a business loan to buy the property when the elderly woman who had lived there moved to residential accommodation. They had carefully thought through how to renovate the bungalow, including the garden, to make it attractive, safe and warm for families. Val still felt such a sense of pride in how she, Olivia and Miriam had brought their dream to reality.

It meant that when Grace came for the initial meeting about Joe, they could sit in a relaxed lounge and she could nurture Grace with tea and cake. Val always saw that as the very first step in creating the warm, supportive team that would be necessary for work with the child to be successful.

She could see Grace viewing The Cottage with approval – and if a professional gave the approving look to her set-up, then Val was already predisposed to being open to that professional. So, despite the picture that Grace painted of a very violent and aggressive six-year-old, Val found herself readily agreeing to assess Joe to see what she might be able to offer. She decided to start by meeting the foster carer, Nickie, and then observing Joe in school before setting up a formal MIM here at The Cottage.

Val arrived at the school early. The receptionist said that the Head was still in assembly. Val asked if she could sit in the hall. The receptionist was a bit wary. A stranger wanting to see what was happening in everyday school life? But Val's DBS and CV were impeccable, so she felt unable to say no.

Val slipped into the hall and sat on a spare chair. It was close to the front of the hall and she could see the wide expanse of young faces, eyes all drawn to the head teacher. She was talking about Halloween, which was just around the corner. Val allowed her gaze to pan slowly over the pupils.

They tended to stand out, the ones referred to Val. At least they stood out to her. It would probably take a scientifically accurate measurement to determine that minuscule additional distance the other children managed to put between themselves and those Val worked with. And how could you measure the intensity that comes from the tightness with which they hold their stomach muscles and the flaccidity of their pelvic floor? It brings about an odd collapse through their body which they balance out with a head-thrusting defiance.

The child was over the other side of the room at the end of a row near a member of staff. The rocking was barely perceptible. One hand pushed down hard under a buttock, the other moving from mouth to knee then towards other children.

Val leant over to a staff member near her. "Who's that?" she asked.

"Jo," replied the teacher.

So, I was right! Val thought in triumph. It was the child she had come to see. The child then turned, and Val saw that it was a little girl. The Joe who had been referred to her was a boy.

Female Jo made piercing eye contact with Val. She felt a catch in her breath and, unbidden, she thought about Mary taking her baby to the temple to be dedicated and being told by Simeon that a sword would pierce her heart. Then having to stand at the foot of a cross seeing her son bloodied and tortured to death. Val got a grip on herself. *It's being in a school assembly*, she explained to herself. It brought back all those memories of being at her own school and the heavy Christian emphasis. Why else would she find herself thinking about Bible stories now?

Jo continued to look at Val, and the pain of it caused her to flinch. Val broke off the eye contact. Jo headbutted a member of staff and was removed from the hall, swearing and spitting. It had been such a sudden shift and because she had dropped her gaze, Val only saw the aftermath.

"What is it with Jos?" the staff member near Val whispered. "Our other Joe we don't even bring into the hall. They just blow for no reason."

Val felt her body react to the teacher's words. Everything drained from her eyes down to a weight in the pit of her stomach, leaving her slumped. Val felt that she had abandoned Jo. In that moment, she hadn't been able to hold the pain in that gaze and stay with it. Jo then showed her necessary survival story, punishing and pushing away the grown-ups who dropped her. Guilt, shame, horror, self-disgust. Val had added to the tapestry of neglect that littered the path which Jo's feet were compelled to follow.

Val wanted to be rude to the staff member. How dare she be so dismissive of such distress and pain, but Val knew that she really wanted to say it to herself. She was the one who had dropped the eye contact with Jo, and now there was no hope of repairing that. She who prided herself on understanding such children. Jo had the greatest of reasons to attack a grown-up; Val had abandoned her and condemned her suffering to be borne alone.

From the observation of Joe at school, Val went on to see Milo. Initially, she was distracted by her thoughts about the two Jos she had seen, but then in the work with Milo there was one of those electric moments, those that come out of nowhere. Not really a moment of "meeting" but something very intense.

It started with Milo being challenging. He had been pushing her for sessions, but every time Val tried to help him enjoy that moment of just letting go with Mel, he would find some way to resist. Where were they now? Session eight, she reckoned, not counting the parent sessions with Mel. They'd bypassed the usual pattern of tentative acceptance followed by resistance starting about session six. Milo had presented a sticky mix of compliance and resistance from the outset.

He might throw the ball, just a bit too high, a bit too hard, leaving Val thinking, *did he do that on purpose?* She couldn't be sure and if she called him out, he looked like butter wouldn't melt in his mouth. His face looked all innocent as if his eyes were saying, "What, me? Do something like that? Never!" It was hard to get her head around feeling bullied by a six-year-old child, but that was what it felt like: manipulation, domestic violence, plain rudeness.

Session after session, she found herself having to almost physically and audibly tell herself to hold onto her anger, think about it, digest it. It really felt as though he was trying to make her angry, trying to make her reject him. Her head knew that this was him recreating to his early experience, but her feelings didn't tie up with her thinking – they just reacted to his rejections and put-downs.

She had just reached the point of thinking the work was pointless, going nowhere. She felt all she could do was breath more deeply, decide to stop trying so hard to win him over. "Just be with him!" she heard her supervisor as if she were speaking in her ear. "Find a way to play."

And then it happened, that electric moment.

Maybe all the pieces dropped into the right places for all of them in that space and time.

He was bargaining with her. Val and Milo were standing by a table on one side of the room, Mel was on the other side and chairs were pushed to one side to make space to play. Val was asking Milo to come away from the table and stand by her so he could safely throw a ball to Mel.

"If you go and stand by the chair, then I will throw the ball to you."

"No," Val said, "we are standing here to throw the ball. If you throw it from there, you might bang your arm on the table and that might be a hurt."

Val stepped towards him and took his hand, thinking the additional nurture may regulate him and help him to relax his guard enough to comply.

But he said, "If you don't go and stand over by the chair, I won't let you talk to Mum."

It was said with utter conviction, as if he was certain that this would make both Val and Mel do exactly as he wanted. Val did a double take. This is what it was like for him. Milo was being his birth dad; Mel was Milo as a child. And Val, she was Milo's birth mum. He had known the threats of his dad, threats that said to his birth mum, "If you don't do what I want, then you won't be able to spend time with your baby."

"Ow, Milo!" Val said. He was squeezing her hand so tightly that it was hurting. Val tried to pull her hand away, but the vice-like grip he had on her belied his six-year-old size.

Val started to mimic crying, using her empathy to put herself in the shoes she thought his birth mum might have occupied.

"I don't know what to do. You are hurting my baby and I don't think I can protect her. If I take her away, you will never talk to me again; if I do what you say, you could hurt us both."

Although she was acting the crying, she allowed her body to droop and she could feel, feel so acutely like a catch in the chest, a pain in the heart, a never-can-win stab in the eye. This really hurt.

She suddenly became aware that both Mel and Milo had gone silent. They were both looking at her.

"Why are you crying?" Milo asked.

"I suddenly found myself thinking about your birth mum. I thought she might have felt like that at times, not knowing how to look after you and look after herself when your birth dad wanted his own way."

Milo came away from the table, still holding Val's hand.

"That's a good place for the game," Val said. "We are going to try to throw the ball back and forward twenty-two times." (*Why 22?* she thought to herself. *Where did that come from?* It just felt right, filled her up and eased the ache.)

"Ready, you throw it when I say go. Three, two, one, go."

She felt the grip on her hand ease as he responded to the challenge. She moved away.

The ball came sailing towards her; perfect throw. She caught it.

"One," she said, and threw it back

"Two!" Milo said as he caught it. "I'm throwing it to Mum!"

"Three!" Mel said as it came to her.

The game went on, slowly, carefully throwing and catching, voices counting. Almost hypnotic in its rhythm. At 22 they stopped, exhausted. Val pulled the blanket out of her bag. She didn't have to say what they were doing. It was familiar now. She spread out the blanket. Milo lay down with his feet to his mum so he could see her face. Together, Val and Mel picked him up in the blanket and slowly rocked him from side to side.

"Twinkle, twinkle, little star,
What a lovely boy you are,
Soft black hair and soft, soft cheeks,
Bright brown eyes from which you peep,
Twinkle, twinkle, little star,
What a lovely boy you are."

They put him down gently. The familiarity of the routine was comforting to them. Val wrapped Milo in the blanket while Mel made herself comfortable on the cushions. Val picked up Milo and wrapped like a parcel in the blanket.

"Special delivery, Mum!" Val made her voice deliberately sing-song.

She put the blanket on Mel's lap, and Mel slowly and with delight started to unwrap Milo. A foot. A hand. A few curls. The smile. A whole arm. All of him. Mel couldn't help but kiss him as his whole face emerged, slightly pink and sweaty from being in the blanket. He stretched out over her lap and yawned. Val passed Mel the box containing two marshmallows.

"I bet you can't beat your record from last week. It took you twenty seconds to nibble that marshmallow – that was such a long time!"

Milo rose to the challenge. He lay relaxed in Mel's arms and let her hold the marshmallow while he took the tiniest nibbles, all the time looking to Mel's face, allowing her to slow him down with her smile and her eyes.

Two minutes it took. Two minutes of being alone together even though Val was in the room. They were lost in each other as Mel fed her son with marshmallows and love and holding.

Something had given. Just a little, but it was a good start – nearly a moment of meeting out of electric resistance.

By the time Val had finished the school visit and met with Nickie and agreed the funding, it was a month before it was possible to set up the MIM for Joe. There was a December chill in the air.

She was nervous as she waited for Joe and Nickie to arrive. She always was with any assessment. At least here at The Cottage she didn't have to worry so much about the surroundings or the video or what others might think.

The car pulled into the driveway. Val opened the door ready to welcome Nickie and Joe. She remembered the fierce energy she had seen in him during the school visit, how hard it had been to keep up with him and that sense of him being at the edge of danger. A sense that he seemed to shed like scales, leaving those around him sprinkled with his angst.

Nickie got out and walked around the car. She had parked so that the rear passenger side door was close to the open door of The Cottage. Val was left with the impression that this was a rehearsed move, that Nickie had developed a skill in organising the space to best channel Joe where he needed to be. It reminded her of watching TV dramas that have bodyguards whose eyes are always outwards looking for possible sources of trouble while their bodily actions move their clients to safety.

Once the car door was open, Joe emerged. Val thought it looked like he was sniffing the air. His movements were precise, his limbs held with a fluid tension, an intensity that suggested every part of him was on high alert about being in this new place.

He spotted the open door and made his way towards it. Val didn't see any eye contact or inclination of his being towards Nickie. No sense that she had given approval or reassurance that it was OK to go to this new place. Joe seemed to pay no reference to her at all; it was as if she had to trail in his wake, swiftly locking the car as she hurried after him.

"I need to go to the loo," was the first thing she said, even before Val could introduce herself formally to Joe. Val pointed Nickie towards the bathroom, and then found herself on her own with Joe. She closed the door of The Cottage while Joe just stood there.

The front door of The Cottage opened into the lounge area that served as their waiting room. She leant her back against the door watching Joe, wondering what he would do as they waited for Nickie to return. Weirdly, she felt like the one who was in strange surroundings. It was unsettling.

Joe looked at Val. Val felt... She couldn't really pinpoint what she felt. She took a moment to go inside while still holding Joe firmly in her mind. She dropped her eye contact with him, not submissively, but aware that the intensity was more than expected in these first moments of meeting. His eyes were piercing her, and she kept her awareness of him in her peripheral visual. Bruce Perry came to her mind: *approach the traumatised child as if they are a frightened small animal.* Wildcat was the one that came to Val's mind, but not frightened. There was nothing cowering about Joe. The fear was all hers, alongside a bright and vivid curiosity about this boy. She found herself smiling even though she wasn't looking directly at Joe.

Joe suddenly launched himself at her. She had no choice but to catch him and hold him away from her. She had her hand against his chest to keep him at arm's length. She was convinced that he was going to sink his teeth into her. He curled himself around her hand, digging his nails in. Intuitively, she found herself rolling him down onto the ground, first on his back as if to tickle his tummy and then over onto his front so she could stroke his back. She was shocked. She wriggled her hand out from underneath him while still stroking his back.

I hope this camera is on, she was thinking. *I hope people can see that I'm not hurting him.*

Then there was a sudden realisation that this was play. This was the way Joe knew how to play. In that moment, even with the camera, even in this new strange place, even abandoned (in his eyes) by Nickie, he wanted to play. This spitting, hissing, biting, scratching wildcat kitten was his playful self.

The whole thing felt like it lasted a lifetime. When she played back the video, it was two seconds at the most. Even when watching it back, she found her heart rate increasing and sweat breaking out on her forehead. Fear and play so very closely mixed.

Val found it hard to concentrate on the MIM. She did all the required stuff, the standard nine activities, her being out of the room watching on the video link. For the leave activity, Nickie tried to prepare Joe. She read the card out loud to him.

"It says here 'Adult leaves the child for one minute', so that is what I am going to do, Joe. Can you see that clock? The hands…" But she didn't even finish the sentence and just left.

Joe sat there for about five seconds and then got up, threw the chair onto its side, went to the door and told her to come back in. He point-blank refused to put hats on her and threw off every hat she put on his head. With the feed, he grabbed all the chocolate buttons and stuffed them into his mouth before Nickie could organise how they might feed each other. Nickie was exasperated. It lasted 10 minutes max.

Val showed the video to Grace. As Joe's social worker, she had formal parental responsibility for him; and the MIM had been so bizarre that Val wanted to do a parent feedback session with her as well as a separate one for Nickie. She felt that she needed far more information about Joe's background, more maybe than a foster carer would find helpful to know.

"Did you know I grew up on a farm in Norfolk?" Grace asked.

Val thought she had disguised the fact that her jaw dropped.

"So why would a big black woman with a surname like Olawale not grow up on a farm in Norfolk?" Grace said with a broad smile.

Val held up her hands in mock surrender. "I stand corrected in my white, middle-class, privileged stereotyping."

It was a conversation of levity and kindness, and at the same time both women felt a deep wounding at the reality of the divide that couldn't be eradicated. Val knew that she spoke from a position of dominance, even if she didn't want to.

Grace continued; practice made it appear easy for her to brush off such denials of her identity.

"There were cats on the farm to keep the rats down. Once, one of the mothers was killed by a tractor. There were four of us children and four kittens, so the farmer asked us to bring them up. I loved mine with all my heart, and she loved me, but I don't think I ever really tamed her. She brought me a dead rat when I was ill with glandular fever. My mother went wild. She never came to our house again, but she would come and rub herself against my legs if she saw me in the yard. I haven't thought about her for years, but seeing Joe somehow reminded me of her."

Val thought about this momentarily. It was a story that felt like it fitted, but she wasn't quite sure how at the moment. It reminded her of the impression she'd had of Joe being like a wildcat as he came into The Cottage for the MIM.

"What do you know about how he came into care?" she asked Grace.

Grace told Val the story as she knew it, starting with Joe's mother. She was 19 when she was found to be pregnant. She had a learning disability and didn't know what was happening. She was eight months pregnant when a neighbour complained to the police about the noise next door: shouting and banging. It had been going on for years and the neighbour had reported things to the police so much that they thought she was a nuisance, but this time Joe's mum had bruises on her face.

She wouldn't say what had happened. She said her boyfriend wanted her to live with him and when she tried to leave, her dad had locked her in a cupboard. Grace thought that they had probably threatened to kill her – she said it in a passive voice as if to try to rob it of the awfulness.

Joe was born. Social services watched over things. Joe's grandparents helped his mum, and social workers felt that things were OK, so they closed the case. It was when Joe was three years old that he was found wandering in the street naked in February. His mum had a fractured skull when police visited the house. They found her slumped in front of a cupboard door.

He was malnourished and when the police searched the house, they found what they thought was his bed in the cupboard under the stairs, the cupboard that they found his mum in front of. His mum recovered in hospital slowly and asked after Joe. She was really anxious that he didn't live with her mum and dad. Her language was limited. Grace's voice became even quieter and more monotone. When the police searched the house, they found a video of Joe's mum. They thought it was of her being raped, but they didn't know who the man was. Joe's grandmother opened up briefly to a social worker as they had a coffee at a burger joint, saying that she protected her daughter as much as she could, she put her in the cupboard for safety, giving her food when she could. Back in the home, she changed her story.

"I think," Grace said slowly and tentatively, "Joe's mum tried to protect him. I think her dad broke her skull when she tried to stop him hurting Joe. I think she wanted to leave with the boyfriend but she wasn't allowed to. I think, but I don't know. No one knew. There was nothing we could do. We don't really know what happened to him for those three years. He's had five placements since he was removed. Carers just can't cope with him, but they all seem to love him."

They sat in silence for a moment, absorbing all of that. The implications of the gaps in the story hurt.

CHAPTER FIVE

Oh What a Piece of Work Is Man

"I have of late—but wherefore I know not—lost all my mirth, forgone all custom of exercises, and indeed it goes so heavily with my disposition that this goodly frame, the earth, seems to me a sterile promontory; this most excellent canopy, the air—look you, this brave o'erhanging firmament, this majestical roof fretted with golden fire—why, it appears no other thing to me than a foul and pestilent congregation of vapours. What a piece of work is a man! How noble in reason, how infinite in faculty! In form and moving how express and admirable! In action how like an angel, in apprehension how like a god! The beauty of the world. The paragon of animals. And yet, to me, what is this quintessence of dust?"

William Shakespeare, *Hamlet*

When Nickie came to The Cottage for the parent play session, she was initially unsure. The MIM feedback had been fine at one level, challenging at another. She hadn't been comfortable seeing herself on video and at the same time mesmerised at how she kept adapting, kept shifting, just kept trying to keep connected to Joe.

She wasn't suspicious of this parent demonstration session; she just wasn't clear why she was being asked to come and play herself. Surely it was Joe who needed the work, and needed it soon.

Ever since the MIM, he had been highly anxious; and this had come out in disruptive behaviour at school and rudeness at home. Nickie knew it was anxiety; Val was yet another professional in the stream of professionals trampling through their lives. Each time, she suspected Joe thought it was a signal that he would be moving on, so each time his behaviour dipped as if he wanted to dump the family before they dumped him.

Well I'm not having any of that, Nickie thought. Joe wasn't going anywhere.

She would fight tooth and nail to make sure everything was done to keep him in her family. Val had pointed out some things she could try to do differently at the MIM feedback session last week. She was making a big deal every time she left Joe, and a big deal of greeting him every time she returned even if she was just nipping out of the room to get a cup of tea or to go to the loo. Initially, they had both felt a bit weird doing this, like putting on an act, but she was surprised how quickly it felt natural and enjoyable. She really *was* pleased to see Joe each time; he was a lovely person even if his behaviour often left a lot to be desired. He seemed to now accept the greeting from her and turn to her as if to expect it. Yes, she had to say it was working. She did feel better about him.

As much as she loved Joe, Nickie had been feeling increasingly weary. As a family, they were finding that they were on edge the whole time wondering what might happen next. It was all very well Val saying maybe it was like Joe was letting on how it had been for him in his first family, always on edge, always fearful, always having to be on alert for the next threat. She knew that with her head, but she and the rest of the family were living with it 24/7.

She was surprised how soothing it was to be led into the room and settled onto cushions on the floor, back against a sofa, the atmosphere calm. She relaxed for a moment, but then she felt the need to spring back to alertness. It had been her everyday state for so long now, since Joe had joined the family, that to be quiet and soothed seemed a bit spooky.

"The first thing I will do with Joe is check for hurts," Val said. "I'm going to start by putting dots of lotion on his freckles to count them, as I think looking at his hurts straight away might scare him off." Val took the bottle of baby lotion and flipped up the lid. She sniffed it and held it out to Nickie to smell too. She noted the relaxation on Nickie's face.

"That takes me right back to when Zoe was born!" she said.

"Zoe's your daughter?" Val checked out.

"Yes, she's fifteen now. She is such a delight! I am in awe of how she keeps her focus on her schoolwork and still seems to make space for Joe to play with her. She is amazingly patient with him."

"It sounds like you are very proud of her," Val said.

"Yes," was the response, and Nickie seemed in a distracted, faraway space as Val spotted lotion onto each of the knuckles on her right hand. Holding the hand, Val started to spread out the lotion, smoothing it gently into Nickie's skin.

"Oh lotion, oh lotion on Nickie's hand. It smells so good and feels so grand!" she sang, concentrating on slowing her breath and keeping a strong, smooth pressure on Nickie's hand. She could feel a wobble in Nickie's body, and spirit, and didn't want to look up at her. She didn't want to intrude on the emotion of what was happening in that moment and at the same time she didn't want Nickie to feel abandoned in the emotion that was being stirred up for her.

She stopped her singing but continued to rub in the lotion, massaging Nickie's hand.

With a gentle, low voice she asked, "What are you feeling right now?"

"Emptiness, sadness. It was as soon as I smelt that baby lotion. I could see Zoe so tiny and dependent on me. How I loved her with a passion. And I feel the same about Joe. You touching me, it just tapped into all the sadness I feel about him. I think he suffered so much, some much more than in his report, but he never lets me in to help him with all of that. We are fine as long as I don't ask him to do something he doesn't want to do, then all hell breaks loose."

Val added some more lotion to Nickie's hand and continued to massage it in. Gently, she took Nickie's other hand and started to lotion that, putting dots on each knuckle as she had with the other hand. She didn't say that she had noticed how rough Nickie's hands were, noticing the hurts that were there, she just tended to them.

They didn't need to speak. Val knew she was touching Nickie far more than just at a physical level. She was mindful that she didn't want to go too deep; this was, after all, a play session, and she already knew that Nickie was highly sensitive to Joe's needs. Her intention had been much more educational – to make sure Nickie knew the games she had planned and the reasons behind them. This level of emotion had somewhat caught her by surprise.

She continued to massage Nickie's hands without making eye contact until she heard Nickie's breathing become more even. Then she looked up and smiled.

"You must think I'm a wimp, crying just because I smell baby lotion," Nickie started.

Val held up her hand stopping the line of thought before it took hold. "Whatever was going on for you was important. I am sure it is connected to us understanding Joe more. I think if we carry on with the things I have planned for the first session, then what you feel will really help me to fine-tune the session. I was going to go on from these to beanbag drops. This is a structure activity to help him feel that he can let us take charge of creating safety."

Val guided Nickie into sitting opposite her and she put a beanbag on Nickie's head.

Nickie smiled shyly. "It feels so weird playing like this," she said.

Val smiled. "How do you play at home?"

"With the children?" Nickie asked.

"No," Val replied. "What do *you* play? We don't stop playing just because we are grown-ups; we just play differently. Now, when I go one, two, three, drop! You drop the beanbag into my hands. OK? One, two, threeee… Drop!" She used her voice to inject excitement into the process. "Well done!" she said in her bright Theraplay voice.

Nickie smiled, then smiled more.

Val noticed. "It's funny, somehow you just can't help yourself. You think of course I'm not going to feel a sense of accomplishment dropping a beanbag into another adult's hands, but somehow it just happens. That connective desire is so strong; it is why we work with attachment, because it is such a powerful drive. Let's try this." She puffed out her cheeks and took Nickie's hand in her own. She got Nickie's hands to squash her cheeks until the air came out with a pop. Again, Nickie just couldn't help but smile.

Val took Nickie through the whole session she had planned for Joe and then made her a cup of tea. Throughout the whole session, she had a niggling sensation, kind of like a sneeze that wouldn't happen, an irritation that seemed to tell her that the force of emotion in the room hadn't really been tapped into. She wasn't really sure how to broach this with Nickie.

Nickie, however, had no problem. Whatever had happened in that play session had left her feeling that she could speak plainly to Val.

"I can see how it works. I can see him enjoying it, but I just don't want to do it. I'm sorry, I just can't do it."

The emotion that had been so active in the checking for hurts was very close to the surface again. Val wondered what hurts were running so deep for Nickie that this highly skilled, warm and grounded professional foster carer was in this moment in time overwhelmed. Val put the teas down and sat next to Nickie. It seemed natural to her to take Nickie's hand. It was shaking, and Nickie pulled it away quickly.

"I'm sorry," Val said, suddenly worried that she had overstepped a boundary.

"No, no." Nickie's voice was cracking with emotion. "I'm just a bit raw. I don't know why but ever since Joe came, I've been thinking about… I lost a baby. After Zoe. Miscarried. About twenty weeks – just too young to survive. We never managed to get pregnant again after that. Don't get me wrong, we didn't go into fostering to replace that baby or anything, I've barely thought about her except on anniversaries and things, but since Joe was placed, I can't get her out of my head. I feel like I did then, like the world couldn't go on, but there was no choice. It just had to and I just had to go along with it. I was in a numb blur for weeks – months, maybe." Nickie paused.

Val handed her a cup of tea.

"Thank you," Nickie replied. It struck Val how polite we still managed to be in the face of such a massive loss.

"What do you need?" she asked.

"Time. I think. Someone else to take the emotional kicking from Joe for a bit. I can work it through. But I just need some time."

Val sat back and took a sip of her own tea. Sitting on a sofa performing grown-up displacement activities as if having a drink kept the rawness away. On the floor, doing attachment in games that were touching and caring, they just got underneath the distancing that adult life was so good at supporting. Joe's wounds had opened up the hurts of Nickie's past. If Joe hadn't come into the home, the healing Nickie had carried out would have been just fine. But something particular about the losses suffered by Joe had hit the sore spot again. Nickie knew herself well. When she said she needed time, she was probably right. The first session was already set up here at The Cottage. Nickie would have only been observing that anyway. And after that, Val thought, *I'll talk with Nickie and Grace about moving the work to school so Nickie doesn't have the worry of getting Joe here, and I'll see him on his own for a while. He needs Nickie so much; there is quite a significant bond between them.* She couldn't let that bond break by asking Nickie to do more than she was able at the moment.

"Anguish."

Brenda looked up to see the red kite soaring high up in the sky. It was strange; they didn't seem to call that much here. She remembered walking along Hadrian's Wall last summer and being surprised by a sound only to look up and realise the noise was coming from the same raptors that she saw at home. It was a pleasant memory.

She stood and watched the kite for a while. They enwrapped her, but she didn't think that was why they were called raptors. Sometimes when she was driving, she needed to pull over so she could watch them because she knew her eyes would continually be drawn towards them and not the road. She couldn't remember now when they had started to reappear – first one, then a pair, and now several pairs. From being rare, they were now not exactly an everyday sight but part of normality. For some reason they were a part of normality that, well, enwrapped her, if there was such a word.

She realised the cry had dissipated her anger somewhat; she had barely been aware of how vigorously she had been walking. So, what was really going on with Val? She was one of the most intuitive therapists she supervised.

There were times when she wished she could be like a kite and have a bird's eye view of all that was going on spread out beneath her. Then she would be able to see how things were related. But with her feet on the ground, it was knotty, trying to unpick all the bits: the stuff the child brings, the stuff the parent brings, the stuff the therapist brings – and her too. She was in the mess and mix with all of them.

Val has nous, that way of knowing that Aristotle connected with understanding people at an almost mystical level. That's why these children ended up on her caseload. The tangled-up, knotty, messy children.

Brenda looked at her watch. She needed to start back. It was such a blessing to be able to grab these 10 minutes between sessions to stomp out and clear her head. The clay mud was sticking to her boots, making her feet heavy as she headed back to the garden room she used for her work. Her feet of clay made her smile in contrast to her desire to have her head in the clouds.

"Bloody philosophers."

It was probably just as well not many other people walked this way.

"So, where did that come from?" she asked herself, still hoping there were no stray dog walkers around. Sometimes Brenda startled even herself with what emerged from her mouth. She had learnt to trust her spontaneous eruptions as a place to start to make sense of the things she didn't know but knew she needed to know.

She liked philosophy but hated it as well. Val couldn't do "I-It" but could be overwhelmed by the "I-thou" if she didn't pace her connection. She tuned into the children, but then couldn't make sense of the overwhelming nature of what came at her. What was the point of describing what might be going on though, if that didn't actually help her to help Val to help Milo and Joe?

"Well, Mr Buber, who else do you think I should ask?" Brenda put out to the universe. It was as if something was just on the edge of her knowing, but she couldn't quite grab hold of it to pull it into focus; and the more she turned to look at it, the less visible it was. But visible wasn't the right word – this wasn't about knowing by seeing. It seemed to be more about knowing by feeling or bodily sensing.

She'd returned to her garden gate and started to scrape the mud from her boots, looking up to see if she could still see the kite. She couldn't see it now, or hear it. Anguish – why did it sound like the kite was saying that?

Brenda intended to look up philosophers she thought might help ground herself and guide her through the complicated thoughts she was having about Val and her work with Milo and Joe. There were a few she thought may be helpful – people who had spent time wondering about how the body helped you find knowledge. She wanted something that would make a bridge between the feelings that engulfed Val and ideas or thoughts that might help them both process the hurts of the children Val was seeing. But in the end, she found herself looking at the story of how red kites were introduced to the Chilterns.

Persecuted because of a myth that they would take lambs, they were driven to near extinction in the area. However, new birds brought in from Portugal established themselves, and now there were more kites than could be tracked. Interesting, but not what she set out to do. *Time for a cup of tea*, she thought, finding yet another distraction from what she thought she should be doing.

With tea made for herself and Edward, she went out to the converted barn that her husband used for his business. She paused briefly to watch through the window as he ran his hand over the sanded wood of the shaker-type chair he was making. She knew he was just checking for smoothness, but the movement was sensuous and utterly absorbed. She loved watching Edward work.

She gently pushed open the door to the workshop and said softly, "Tea?" not wanting to break the reverence of his work but also wanting that feeling for herself.

"Hi! Yes. Thanks. How's it going?" It was as if Edward pulled himself back along a tunnel from absorption in the work to being present with Brenda.

"Fine. How is the chair coming along?"

A smile spread through Edward. It may have been his face that showed the emotion, but the radiance of the experience was somehow expressed through the whole of his body. He couldn't stay away from the wood, stroking it, smoothing it. The beauty of his movements brought her near to tears. She felt it like a hard lump in her chest, a hold of longing, of knowing and not knowing. She wanted the certainty of his working; she didn't have it, and that made her sad.

Later that day they were sitting together.

"Tell me about the chair?" she said.

Edward looked at her, puzzled. "I don't know what to say."

"How did you decide what to do, what wood to use…? I don't know – you just look so much like you know what you're doing."

Edward mused. "It just happens. I work at it and it emerges." But he seemed bemused by his own words.

The first pieces of furniture he'd made after leaving the bank were serviceable. Now they were beautiful, yet he didn't know how they had moved from one to the other. There had been terrible mistakes on the way and he had abandoned things that had started in such promising ways. There had been despair and the thought that he should never have left the security of the mundane day-to-day of work in the financial sector, but then there were the moments when it just all seemed to come together.

"I don't really know what I do."

The reality was that he got up every morning and went to the workroom and worked until it was time to stop. He looked at books and thought about nothing in particular and sometimes he took a day off to go and see how other people made things.

"I suppose it is a bit like meditating; you get into the zone."

Brenda shook her head with a sort of exasperation. How did this help? But something in her said there was a connection, something that would make it possible for her to help Val make sense of the loss of faith she seemed to be suffering.

Loss of faith? Was that what it was?

"You know by doing," Edward said, and it sounded from his voice that he was being sucked back down his tunnel.

"Doing what?"

"Making it," Edward replied and got up to return to the workshop.

Knowing how distressed Val had been at their last supervision, Brenda had arranged to see her again. Val had seen Joe between the supervisions, and his liveliness had taken the edge off the difficulty of the place she had been to in her last supervision.

Brenda was determined, however, to see if there was learning to be gained.

"Tell me about being stuck," she said to Val.

"This whole thing is so painful," Val said. "I just don't know what is going on. I read things, and they all make perfect sense when I read them. I think all things have their time and decide in my head to wait for the meaning to emerge from the work, but I just can't face it."

Val seemed more bemused than hurt, as if she was holding her breath in anticipation of something. Brenda was reminded of the pain of hopeful anticipation that she had felt watching Edward sanding the chair, the "on the cusp of knowing" sense. But she didn't think Val was there. This was a more primitive, out-of-touch feeling of being lost.

"Can you tell me anything about what is going on at the moment?" she asked.

Val just sat with her eyes on a spot on the floor. For a moment, Brenda wondered if she had actually heard what she'd said. Then it was as if the words were dragged out of her.

"I just don't know."

Brenda remembered Edward saying, "Making it." The action being the mechanism that showed what was there, that provided knowledge of what the material was becoming.

She found herself thinking, *if this was Theraplay, what would we need now? Movement, embodiment, play. We need to engage so there is something, anything to connect to. We need to make something.* Without some sort of playful engagement with Val, she could feel anger starting to stir within herself, anger at herself for her stupid question and anger at Val. Val seemed so vulnerable. Brenda took a sharp intake of breath. Val was vulnerable and she, Brenda, felt angry with her. That was not what she wanted to feel – but she was.

What a mess. What a muddle. She wanted to bail out. She wanted to return to the soothing serenity of the craft shop with her husband making glorious, solid, beautiful chairs.

So, what did they need to make?

They sat in disconnected silence. Going nowhere, doing nothing. Brenda felt there was nothing she could do but sit with it. She felt as though her whole being was forced up into her head, and it took a focused stream of thought to move her attention back to her whole body.

There was only one thing for it, she had, herself, to find some way to play. The red kites came back to her mind: destruction, misunderstanding, near death, return to life, thriving.

"Anguish," she heard herself say.

"Sorry?"

"It's what the kites seem to say to me. When I walk and hear them. The red kites, the birds." She added, seeing the puzzlement on Val's face, "You have no idea what I'm talking about, do you?"

CHAPTER SIX

Initial Engagement, Tentative Acceptance

It was eleven weeks in now, two parent sessions, and now the eleventh Theraplay session. Week by week the sessions with Milo continued. Largely, they played the same games to give Milo that sense of continuity and predictability. He became familiar with them. Mel started to know what to expect and was able to take a lead in the activities. Milo didn't exactly seem to enjoy them, but when Val suggested doing a weather report at home as part of his bedtime routine, they both seemed happy enough with the idea. Mel reported that the bed-wetting was much less, and the tantrums less, and her sense of perpetual anxiety less, and she felt Milo seemed less ready to seize on anything that was out of the ordinary and react with overwhelming anxiety which came out as rage. It was the way she said it that made Val think it was all still somewhat overwhelming at a deep, unthinkable level.

Val thought the session reminded her a bit of the meeting at County Hall. It was going well, but there was a lack of passion about the whole thing. There were those flashes such as when Mel really got what was going on in the MIM and was ready to work, or that session where Milo let go a little and let himself be nurtured by Mel. But overall, Val had the sense that there was a huge holding back and reservation about the whole thing in Milo.

For a parent session in mid-December, Milo's dad, Simon, was able to join them. It wasn't often that he was able to get away from work. Val had that sense there was something on their minds, and it was Simon who spoke first.

"Louise is badgering us about the adoption order. She wants to know if we are ready to put in for the final hearing."

"And are you?" Val asked.

"Well," Mel said hesitantly, "Milo's certainly come a long way, but I don't really feel that he has fallen in love with us yet and—" she took a deep breath and the next bit came out all in a rush "—what if it all goes wrong and we are on our own and social services don't give us the help they have promised and…"

Simon took her hand to try and slow her down.

"We are just not sure what we should be asking for to make sure they don't leave us in the lurch."

For two strong, confident professionals who also happened to be adoptive parents, Mel and Simon looked awfully small and vulnerable on the sofa where they sat. Had they really lost weight and shrunk since Milo had come to live with them? Or was Val picking up on how they felt diminished at some level by the experience of parenting Milo.

She reviewed the treatment goals with them; they could acknowledge that Milo was more compliant and less aggressive. They could see that he wet the bed less often and it didn't seem such an aggressive act. They could acknowledge that he seemed to be settled at school and although he hadn't been invited to any parties, he seemed to have a growing group of friends. He hadn't wanted to join the school football team, but he seemed to enjoy having an informal kick around with his classmates in the park as they walked back from school together. Although, Mel was very aware that as she and the other mothers chatted while the boys played, the mums seemed to keep a close eye on Milo, carefully positioning themselves and their pushchairs to face the area of play, often leaving Mel with her back to the activities. That meant she was never sure how much Milo was to blame for the bumps and scrapes and heavy tackles that he seemed to be accused of. Yes, it seemed to be going well, if a little joylessly.

They thought together about what Mel and Simon really wanted post adoption. What would make them feel safe and secure? They wanted to know that they could access therapy whenever they felt Milo needed it and that someone would also be there to help them. Val suggested they write down what it was they were asking for so they wouldn't forget. She found Mel's thoughts flitted to the physiotherapy exercises that had been suggested to help Milo with his coordination and the speech therapy exercises they needed to do, and keeping in mind the community paediatrician who was going to carry out the LAC/adoption medical. Val reassured them that some red tape activities would end when the adoption was finalised. It seemed to be this that swayed them to put in for the final hearing – the thought of getting so many professionals out of their, and Milo's, lives so they could try and focus on just being a family.

Session one, Joe was under the chair in the waiting room. It was the only one they were going to do at The Cottage. Joe kept swearing at her, leaving Val with a mixture of feelings – scared and amused – so she started to use swear words, too. Val guessed her feelings might be a mirror of Joe's.

Miriam happened to be in there catching up with some case notes and came through to see what the commotion was. Wanting to be helpful, she suggested Nickie come with her to the therapy room. Val could see that Miriam expected Joe to follow. But to follow your carer you have to be attached to them, want to keep a proximity to them. Val's gut said that wasn't going to happen for Joe. So, she lay on the floor close to him.

Joe kept coming up with new words, and in the end Val said to Nickie, "Wow, he's brilliant. Did you know he knew so many swear words?"

"If you want to know someone who knows lots of swear words you should ask my dad," Joe responded. He then came out from under the chair and walked to the therapy room, just like an "ordinary child". The waiting room hellion was gone.

In the therapy room, Joe slumped on the floor, as far away as he could from Val. It was a perfect set-up for Theraplay: pretty bare, not that big, very little furniture, but lots of comfortable cushions and a soft flooring. Val did a "check-up" from a distance.

"He's got a great hairstyle, hasn't he?" Val said to Nickie. "I bet he has brought really strong arms with him too."

She got out the bubble mix and blew bubbles. Joe tried very hard not to be interested, but it looked like there was a battle going on inside him between "I'm not going to let you care about me" and "I really want to play" inner states. He fidgeted and looked for his foster carer's bag. Val guessed he wanted to find her phone and distract himself with a game, avoiding the playing together. Val had asked Nickie to put her bag in the video room before the session started. Joe knew the video was recording the session. He also knew where the bag was, and Val could see him getting restless.

She stood up so that she could blow the bubbles better and also move closer to the door. If he was going to bolt, she wanted to be between him and the door so he couldn't get out. Val got Nickie to start popping bubbles by poking them with her index finger.

"I bet you can't pop these bubbles faster than I can blow them." Val didn't even really say it directly to Joe. It was more of an invitation to him and his foster mum together.

In the end, he couldn't resist; and his speedy popping with flailing arms helped him to express some of his agitation.

"Do you reckon you could do it with your elbows?" Val said. The game went on until Val said, "I bet you and Nickie can't high-five them between you and pop them that way?"

They could. Joe was wreathed in smiles and then realised what was happening. He was having fun. Connecting with his foster mum. Furious, he ran at Val. She wrapped her arms around him and sidestepped, swinging him around in a full circle.

"Wheeeee!" she said with pleasure in her voice. When his feet reconnected with the ground, Val said, "I have three rules when I play with people: no hurts, have fun and stick together. That's a great game and to make sure we have no hurts, let's do it this way." She picked up a very large cushion and said, "OK, now run at me – the cushion will stop either of us getting hurt."

He didn't run, but he did push hard against the cushion, enraged, and then just sat on the floor. Val praised him for being so strong and said that she thought he was probably tired now. Val got his foster mum to measure his fingers with strawberry bootlaces saying it would be a chance for Joe to rest and refuel. Nickie measured around his arm, admiring his muscles, then measured his smile. Each time, she gave Joe the bootlace lengths of sweet to eat. He couldn't resist the sweetness, nor could he resist the relationship that came with it.

He looked at Val as if to ask, "What *is* this about." All his usual strategies to alienate the adults so they would reject him hadn't worked here, and they hadn't talked about his "bad behaviour" once.

When it was time to leave, Val realised why Nickie was so precise about managing the process of getting Joe from one spot to another. To underline the fact that it had been unsettling to him, a grown-up enjoying being with him was so far beyond his expectations of the world, he did a runner between the front door of The Cottage and the car. Embarrassed and feeling a bit helpless, they phoned Grace, falling into that place of, without thinking, hoping her parental responsibility would somehow magic up the answers of how to manage him.

Knowing where The Cottage was situated, Grace was really laid back and said to just wait until he returned: there was nowhere to go, no other houses close by, no dangerous road, nothing he could get into trouble with. And if he didn't come back before dark, then to phone the police. Nickie and Val looked at each other. It was all very well Grace saying that, but Val had other clients to see and Nickie was terrified about what her supporting social worker would say about such a plan.

Miriam came out of the front door and suggested they go back into the kitchen. She had been baking a cake in between writing her notes. It was just out of the oven and cooling when Joe came through the back door. She

45

had given him a huge slice without saying anything and then locked the back door while he sat down to eat it.

Disaster averted.

Val felt such relief in that moment. She would carry out her work with Joe at his school. It would be far less stressful because she would be able to share the responsibility of managing Joe with others.

It was just the next week that Joe's work started in school. After the first session, Val felt Joe was such a handful that she wanted to understand how to engage with him first, before having to split her attention to support Nickie in understanding how to be an active part of the Theraplay alongside her. Nickie heard this as she could step out of sessions completely, not as Val had intended, that Nickie would sit and watch. The relief on Nickie's face was so clear that Val just went along with the misunderstanding and worked with Joe on her own. She found the sessions exhausting but strangely exhilarating. She wasn't sure quite what therapeutic progress was being made, other than she found herself increasingly looking forward to seeing him.

He was beautiful. There was something about Joe that took Val's breath away. Later, she tried to think what it was. He had exceptional eyes. It would be easy for his look to be uncomfortable. It just didn't waiver. It was as if it pinned you down.

Why could she tolerate, even value, that experience? Why was that steady, cold "holding the look" unnerving for other people, while for her it said he was a boy who could be rescued?

She cringed at the word "rescue". Joe didn't believe he needed rescuing. For him the world was just fine. It had always been just fine. He had always been able to control the world by his look. His look could cause bad men to go to prison. His look could make his grandad stop beating his mother. At least in his mind it could. In his mind, at least, he had rescued her. He wasn't sure that he gave his grandad that look because he wanted to rescue his mum; in the mind that he had grown into, that was the place she inhabited, her function. The thing, the really important thing, was that it was him looking. When he did that look, he felt like he existed.

The scary bit, the unsafe bit, was when he was looked at.

To be seen.

For Joe, that was the pits. Once you were seen, you just didn't know what might happen next, and inevitably it wasn't good. But what was good? The people he was with now didn't seem to know what good was. Not like he did.

Joe felt his insides squirm as this woman looked at him. He fixed her with his look. He was waiting for her to drop her eyes. That's what they all did when he looked. It was good. It meant they didn't see him.

But she didn't break eye contact. She just kept looking. She said she wanted to play with him.

She couldn't be trusted. She wouldn't get near him; he wouldn't let her get near him! He screamed and screamed. He ran to the end of the room. She kept talking. He wanted her to go away but she wouldn't. He ran to the door, but she was already there. She stood with her back to it.

He could feel things cracking. It was too much. Far too much. She just wouldn't go away. But weirdly, in that moment, he didn't hate her. Whatever it was, he didn't want to disintegrate her. It was as though, in his chest, two channels were running at once: The one that screamed and screamed and screamed and stared and spat and bit and wanted her to go and thought, *so cruel. How cruel. Let me out.* And another, newer channel that was curious about why, why, why, why did she not go?

It was beyond anything he had experienced before. The fact that her voice didn't change, that she didn't let him go, yet she was not scared of him. He felt something. He didn't know it was curiosity. Something felt safe – safe enough to wonder about some other possibility. He didn't see that Val had tears in her eyes. After that session, she just sat in the room, the debris of the session around her. She could barely muster the energy to clear up.

Week 4: "Joe, stop!" The TA bellowed down the hallway. Joe didn't take a blind bit of notice. He ran straight at Val. She had just enough time to drop her bags and move the trolley to one side. Joe leapt up against her, and she had no choice but to wrap her arms around him. Instinctively, she moved her head back. She remembered when she first started this kind of work and a child excitedly leaping up, catching her under the chin and giving her concussion. *Who needs a gym session with weights to keep yourself trim when there is Theraplay?* she thought.

"Hi, Joe," she said. "I am really pleased to see you too. Now, I think Mrs Potter needs you to go back to her so you can show her how you can walk down the corridor."

He didn't resist her putting him down on the floor, and he gave her the most knowing and devilish grin as he ran back down the corridor to Mrs Potter. He then minced his way back at a walking pace and as they arrived said, "Mrs Potter, I walked down the corridor, can I have my sticker now?"

That had been the deal. Mrs Potter looked like she was sucking a lemon to keep her words in; she had been bested and she knew it. She forced out, "Which one do you want?" through gritted teeth. Val couldn't help but smile in recognition. She made a mental note: Mrs Potter could do with some time to talk about how Joe was impacting on her – the delightful, irritating, confusing, feeling-evoking charmer that he was.

"Joe, give me five minutes to set up the room," she said, "then Mrs Potter will bring you along for your session." She gave Mrs Potter an encouraging wink as she gathered the bags and the trolley of cushions and floor coverings to trundle off down the corridor to the room they used. Once there, she moved the desks to one side, stacked the chairs, set up the video and made a comfortable corner for Joe with blankets laid out on the floor and cushions against the wall to support him.

Those meetings with school staff were vital. Joe was energetic and caused mayhem, but he was happy. Mostly. And when he wasn't, he radiated whatever feelings were inside him. People who cared about Joe, and wanted to understand him, just "felt it". The intensity of those emitted feelings was such that sometimes they felt as if they were their own. They were left with strange experiences, very strong feelings, and Val found that part of her work was to give some space for them to decompress, like Mrs Potter.

When Val caught up with her later, she cried.

"I don't know why I am crying!" she said. She found herself laughing at herself at the same time, and then she hiccupped and looked exhausted. Val helped her to talk until Mrs Potter's talk became about her daughter and her new grandchild. When Val saw the broadness of the smile on Mrs Potter's face, she knew that she had processed the distress that Joe had projected on to her.

It was hard to deeply empathise with what Joe's distress was. He didn't really know himself, and what he did project was so raw, undigested and primal. Val could only trust her sense, her best professional guesses based on his story and her years of experience. She had learnt to take seriously, at a visceral level, the difference in herself in the presence of a distressed child. Emotions and thoughts trailed after.

If she could see inside Joe's head, what would be there? She always thought in the present tense when she tried to work it out.

Sometimes he wonders about his mum and dad, and it is painful. He feels like he is falling apart if he rests. Sleep is horrible. As he feels his body relax, it's as though he is falling into nothingness – a pit with no bottom that engulfs him until his whole body jumps him back into life, as if his mind is acting like a mental defibrillator.

What would happen if he just let go?

Val found herself thinking about a book she had read about artic explorers – how a person gets so cold, tired and lacking in food that they just give up. Or pictures she had seen of babies in orphanages in old communist countries – dead in all but body and marasmus that carries on even if food is supplied.

The immediacy of the present tense came back to Val. Joe has to buzz himself so he knows he's alive. I am scared or I am angry or I am fizzing like a shaken bottle of pop, therefore I AM. Is that what was going on for Joe? Thinking isn't enough to know that I AM. Thinking, for Joe, probably means "I am not" because if I think, the awfulness of the pain and the hatred and the pure terror would be so much that I would just explode. This explosion would have no words, just horror. Val shook her head to remove herself from the sense of reverie she had fallen into. For a moment, she hadn't known where she began and Joe ended.

I remember, Joe thinks. But maybe he doesn't, maybe this is what someone thinks he remembers. Something they then wrote down so it became a truth. Val couldn't even remember if the story was something she'd read in his paperwork, or something Nickie said had been told to her at a contact meeting, or something that just seemed to gather, wraith like, out of the air.

The cat was put in the washing machine. It was decapitated, and they laughed when he tried to glue its head back on with superglue. Or maybe he remembers a doll, or a child dismembered, or not? Too much. The cat — that could be it. If it were a girl it would be unthinkable, but there is a thought.

Miss Yates had spoken to Val after she'd asked the class to draw pictures of their pets. Joe looked as if the weight of Old Father Time had fallen on his shoulders, she'd told her. Our pets was the topic. He draws the cat with a head and a body separated.

Miss Yates said, "That's lovely, Joe, but the head should be on the cat."

When she spoke to Val, she said, "He then just threw the chair at me. Why did he do that? I was saying he had drawn a good cat." She looked very pale.

"Are you OK?" Val asked.

"Just queasy. Morning sickness. It just goes on all day." Actually, it didn't, it was the only way she could make sense of why she felt so sick talking to Val about the picture of the cat and Joe's response.

Joe was suspended for his unruly behaviour and the cat haunted him in the night. He got up when everyone was asleep. He didn't know. No one knew. It was as though his body went on autopilot, a ghost walker that seeks out glue. When Val heard about the night-time incident she guessed, deep in his soul, something was saying, "I want to make it all right; I want to make good the irreparable. I want my cat back. Its warmth. The way it sat against me and was there."

Nickie was baffled when she tried to open the washing machine door the next day. Joe completely denied he'd glued the washing machine door shut. He totally knew it wasn't him. He'd been in bed all night. Slept like a log. But the evilness he knew that defined him was gnawing at his stomach. He hadn't saved it, her, anyone. His look had failed him.

Val went back to read the notes. It helped, sometimes, to be reminded of the details. The incoherent pieces of the jigsaw puzzle of everyone's feelings could suddenly fall into place.

Joe was three when he was removed from his birth family. No one even knew the family had a cat; maybe they didn't. Cats go missing all the time in that area. New ones are just born because no one does anything to prevent it. It wasn't the first time a dismembered cat had turned up on a doorstep. The police thought it might have been foxes. There was a story about one that had glue around its neck that was found on the back doorstep of the house when the police rescued Joe and his mother. That one was different. That wasn't a fox. It was just an incidental detail in a bigger horror story. No one investigated it further. And if Joe was only three, he couldn't really speak, so his memory wouldn't recall it as a clear event, would it?

Val sat there, her head spinning. What was true and what wasn't? Or what sort of truths were true? Or not? And who knew anyway? She felt like she was opening her eyes underwater, wanting to see but feeling the salt or chlorine sting, and then being seized by the terror of needing to breath and thinking she couldn't. Was this how it was to be Joe?

CHAPTER SEVEN

Resistance is Fertile

"One word that was never spoken.
One light that was never lit up.
An unparalleled confusion.
And a road without end."

Carl Jung, *The Red Book*

Relationships take time. Session nine, session ten, session eleven, parent session; session twelve, session thirteen. The pattern was settling.

Staff at the school were being great. She had taken time to chat with the reception team, explaining enough of what she was doing to help them understand, but not saying so much that Mel might feel her privacy was being broken if they said something to her. Each week she moved desks to one side of the room and made a cosy corner with cushions and a rug for Milo and Mel. Each week she moved the desks back. Each week she made sure she cleared up any cotton wool scraps from the carpet. Each week she prepared her list of activities carefully, watching the video back from the last session and thinking about what goals Mel wanted for Milo.

"I just want him to love me!" was the main one.

"And how would you know that?" Val had asked Mel at the parent session.

"I'd just know!" Mel had said in exasperation. "I don't know what it would look like, I'd just feel it. At the moment, I just feel sick in the pit of my stomach whenever we have to come to your sessions."

Relationships take time, Val repeated to herself aware, even in her silent voice, that there was a hardening of tone. The school was receptive, and she softened towards them. *Milo and Mel?* Val's mouth pulled into a straight line and she heard herself grunt a little as her breath left her in a rush. She sighed, deliberately a little more softly. Anger. Sadness. Anger. Sadness. The flip-flop of emotion from one to the other was wearing.

She looked at her watch. The desks were moved. The rug and cushions set out. She checked the camera. Checked her bag of equipment. Checked her list of activities pinned to the wall. Checked inside herself – yes, she was delaying and avoiding. It was time to go back to reception to collect Mel and then to collect Milo from his class.

So, what did she want from today's session? Probably not that much different to Mel, except as a professional she couldn't really call it love. She had written down "increased eye contact – shown by at least five occasions of direct eye contact sustained so both parties are aware eye contact has been made" and "Mum to be able to physically regulate Milo – shown by Mum initiating physical contact during energetic games". After 11 sessions, the games would now be familiar to Milo, so today she felt able to focus more on the relationship she wanted to construct with him. She called his face to her mind and in doing so, felt herself mellow a little. She started the video camera so she didn't have to think about switching it on as they returned, and then left the room to fetch them.

Milo, keen to leave class, had run ahead of them to the room. Mel wanted to tell Val that the dog was avoiding Milo, but that Milo would go and find Sophie. It wasn't really that he was tormenting her, but Sophie would take his attention for a while and then get up and go away, seeking Mel out as if to say "make him leave me alone".

The structured entry Val had planned just didn't happen. They were going to take giant moon walking steps into the room with the two of them swinging Milo between them. Instead, he was already in the room and taking everything out of her bag.

Val wasn't sure what was rising in her – maybe it was everything and all at once. She was enraged and terrified that Milo was systematically taking apart the bag of activities that she had so carefully and kindly put together for him. Terrified, of what? Of whom? The terror was so constricting that she didn't know the direction of the terror, just that it was all-consuming and dismissible all at once. What, after all, could she be afraid of in a small boy who, if she needed to, she could just pick up?

"Oh, Milo," she said, "you've found the first activity!" But her voice sounded full of false jollity to her. She didn't feel joy; she wanted to shout at him and tear him off a strip for not complying. Where did that come from?

She needed to move. She wasn't sure where the impulse came from, but she just knew it.

"If you're happy and you know it, clap your hands," she started to sing. "If you are happy and you know it, clap your hands." She continued thinking, *I am so not happy.*

But the song carried on singing for her. Milo and Mel were not joining in, but she felt herself calm a bit, felt a genuine smile starting to take root on her face and felt her breath deepen, filling her more. Milo, at least, had stopped pulling everything from her bag.

As she continued to sing, she gently removed the cotton balls from his hands and put the lotion back into the bag. "We'll get to use those later on," she sang. "We'll get to use those later on. First, we do our check-up, and then you'll really know you're ready, then you'll know you're really ready for our games."

They were both looking at her – well, that was something. Although, she wasn't sure that she liked what she read on their faces. Best not to think. Press on.

She had planned a check-up with lotion and cotton balls. Mel had been learning this technique over the last few sessions and they had talked it through in the parent session, trying to move from a focus on what to do with the cotton ball and lotion towards a sense of why to do it. Mel was due to lead it this week, but there was a stunned silence in the room. Both Mel and Milo looked shocked, like they couldn't move.

Val could see that she needed to get their social engagement systems going. Was it her who had sent them into a state of fear? Or had she made a safe enough space for the fear and trauma to come out? She didn't think so. She had felt immobilised by fear until she started to sing. *Rhythm and movement might*, she thought, *co-regulate them.*

"Head, shoulders, knees and toes," Val started. She pointed to her own. "Head, shoulders, knees and toes," she sang, pointing to Mel's. "Ears and eyes and mouth and nose." This time the focus was on Milo. She took his unresisting hands and put them on his head. "Head, shoulders, knees and toes."

She stopped, and the silence in the room was intense. The radiator gurgled and Val felt herself jump. She realised that as soon as she had stopped singing, she had also stopped breathing. This was fear. Did she name it? Or just play? Would the play help them all come off high alert and make sense of the fear? She dropped inside herself for a moment. She couldn't name it. She had to trust whatever came. They needed to be on the floor.

"I bet you can't do this," she said to Milo. She lay down on her back and curled up into a ball. "I'm going to be a starfish," she said as she unfolded herself until she was spread out like an X on the carpet.

"That's easy," Milo responded, and he lay on his back curled up. He struggled to unfurl himself, his arms happening first, then one leg, then the other.

"Can you curl up again, like a starfish escaping a whale?"

He pulled in one limb after another, panting with the effort of it, but Val felt the knot in the pit of her stomach ease a bit. Mel still looked stunned.

"Let's all be starfish and see if we can stick together." Maybe that would help to integrate something of an underdeveloped Moro reflex.

Val almost had to help Mel to the floor. Milo's movements were becoming more fluid with his curling and unfurling, but it was challenging to tune into his timing. It was also impossible to sing with her core working that hard.

As Milo unfurled again, before he could tense his muscles to recurl, Val said, "Let me see how floppy you are."

He looked so vulnerable spread out on the floor with his arms and legs out, and so uncomfortable. He couldn't let go; he couldn't allow his feet and hands to just hang on the ends of his limbs.

Mel rolled onto her side. "This is more like a gym class!" she said. Val was relieved to hear her speak; the silent stickiness that had overcome her had lifted. Her tone of voice sounded genuine.

"Mum, you take Milo's feet," Val said. "I'm going to take his hands. We are going to help him curl up like a starfish…"

Milo couldn't let them guide his hands and feet, but they were able to keep hold of them.

"And uncurl to spread out and feel at home…" Adding a bit of story seemed to make it seem a bit less intense for him – not really part of the core Theraplay protocol, but a necessary adaptation for Milo's trauma response to whatever was going on in the room that day. "And curl up to protect yourself."

Val wondered if Milo was starting to feel relationship, and that it was unbearably frightening because it made him feel vulnerable. He had to resist vulnerability, so had to resist relationship. That was his necessary life of survival. Move away from the threat; make the threat move away from you.

It had been such a tricky start to the session, with her plan just not fitting the need. Val had been feeling wobbly and she wanted her structure to help her feel safe. She needed to know she was good at this, needed to know that she was making a difference to the lives of the people she worked with. Val had been throwing herself into reading and researching, trying to find out what she should be doing to help Milo deal with his early history and the relational trauma that he had been exposed to. Theraplay was such a good model when adapted for trauma. So, she was doing just that. Her head was telling her that she was doing just that.

At one level, it was going through the motions: Beanbag drop, change the tempo to catch his interest, adapt and mix up the games. Get that tone of voice, tune into him, tune into Mel, tune into herself.

For a while, Val lost herself in the actions. She forgot what she was meant to be doing. In the here and now, she just worked out how to balance the beanbag, enjoyed the feel of Milo's hair on her hand, the way he tilted his head in concentration to keep the beanbag there. Her unthought "oooh" as he managed to take Mel's hand to brace himself and make it possible to keep the bag in place until she said "drop". The unthought, unselfaware "wow!" as it landed in her hands. It wasn't him doing, or her doing, or anyone doing at all. The wonder of it, the wonder of just being together came upon them all. She didn't think; she took Milo's hands and looked deep into his eyes and they were both unguarded.

She truly, truly looked at him. She could look now because she was no longer caught in a defensive position in response to his terror. It was shocking. Seeing into his soul like that meant he was also seeing into her own soul. It was as though they burnt each other. It was only going back and watching the video that she was able to remember what had happened.

He knew she knew. Need, with anguish. The red rawness of suddenly feeling wanted when you knew with every cell that the true story was of being unwanted, discarded, obscene in being. Daring to even contemplate another story? Val had words for it; Val had therapeutic methods to define it. She had years of language-based therapy during her training. She had supervision. All of it kept the illusion of her doing all right, but this little boy in this little moment saw through it all. She was nothing. She felt sick to her stomach.

Her back was to the camera, so when she later viewed the tape, she wasn't sure if she went white; she felt like she had. His face – it was so difficult to really know from the video. His face stilled, slackened. It was similar to what they'd witnessed during the MIM: the wanting to but not knowing how. This was more – a deeper distress and confusion. It wasn't about the bodily mechanics of not knowing how to engage, it was having no possible story other than their joint stories of *being wrong*. From the moment of being born they, both Val and Milo, were wrong and had to observe others so strongly that they became the woodwork and wallpaper and fabric of the environment. Show no face, make no meaningful sound, don't breathe, lock it all up in the centre of your chest like a rusty stake through your heart, pinning your front to your back and immobilising you to nothing. To absolute stillness.

To break that frozenness was like falling apart, falling upwards and downwards and in a million directions, an explosive decompression of self.

The necessary alternative was to hold oneself together. Nothing or no one could be trusted to hold the self together.

Val had broken that safety net and left Milo in that still frozen explosion. It was a scream of no sound. And she had done it to him. She hadn't "adapted for trauma". She had burst through his safety door so violently because she had lost herself and put her needs above his without even being aware until it was too late because she thought too much and tried too much and wanted, too, too much, to save him.

That night she had a dream about Milo. He was a tadpole in a lake being chased by shadowy fish that seemed threatening. He moved at the speed of light to get away until he could move no further, and then he turned into a huge, ugly angler fish with menacing protruding teeth. She woke up with a start.

Val wished she could sit Joe down and just get him to say what was in his head. The tension in him was visceral; he was all wire and movement. It felt like he was being torn from the inside, as if the story he held was trying to get out but he just didn't know how.

She thought about the slippery slip game they had played today. The disgust on his face as she covered his hands in lotion was very minimal. When she went back and looked at the video, she wasn't even sure if it was there; it was more of a shadow of an impression left inside her as she reflected on the moment.

She'd held his hands tightly between hers and said excitedly, "I'm holding you; I'm holding you; I'm holding as long as I can..." and then she slipped her hands away, making a big scene of falling over backwards.

Usually, children loved this game, but when she rolled up again, she was struck by Joe's face. It was frozen. She met his eyes – a rare experience, as he was adept at avoiding her gaze. She hadn't realised how blue his eyes were. It was as if they were barely registering as a colour, and they were filled with terror.

"Joe! I'm sorry!" she exclaimed, and then the moment was gone.

He literally shook himself like a dog coming out of a lake of cold water. The restoration of "normality" so quickly after the flash of terror was fascinating to Val. Despite all the awfulness he had experienced, somehow, Joe seemed to have kept hold of a way to process fear, where he knew that the relationship wasn't overtly abusive. Val wanted to think about how different that had been to her experience with Milo, but Joe reached out and grabbed her hands.

"My turn."

As he slipped away, his nails dug into her hands. She was sure it was deliberate.

Her voice overly bright, she said, "We need more lotion on our hands; it was hard to slip away."

While she winced inwardly at her tone of voice, it reminded her of how she had sounded with Milo. She felt pleased he could tell her that he was angry, that she had hurt his feelings, even if he couldn't do it with words.

She would take that to supervision later but, here and now, reflecting on what she was doing while she was doing it, she said, "That hurt. I think you are telling me that I hurt you. Not in your body, but in your feelings. I am sorry I did that."

Trauma seemed to make history keep repeating itself for both Joe and Milo. Bad things happen, good things are taken away and we all carry on as normal. With her false brightness, she had fallen into the same old, same old pattern of let's pretend this is acceptable. If she could have spat at herself, she would have done; it felt like the right thing to do, and she wondered why.

If only they knew both boys' stories – not the official ones in the reports. If only she could have sat them down and they could have told her – my dad spat at me, my dad hit me, my dad pulled my arm until I thought my shoulder would dislocate, my dad hated me and called it love, and my mum just carried on as normal.

Val felt the weight of the whole story – unknown, imagined – burden her. It helped her to imagine the stories to give words to the feeling she had inside. That gave her a verbal structure to stabilise her. She imagined Grace would say, "Be careful; they are inferences only. We don't know the factual truths. They may have emotional truth, but we just don't know."

Val knew that her imagination of Joe's story helped her to think how she wanted to be with Joe and see how she could try to ease the awfulness. The times she did this and could turn the insight into a Theraplay game and then observe him become more connected, then she could infer that her *best professional guesses* were close enough to his truth to be helpful.

Ah truth! One good solid truth would be so lovely and helpful and clear! Like sunshine on new snow. Clear. Pure.

Val rubbed her eyes and massaged the sides of her head. *I need a haircut*, she thought, as if that might make it easier for her head to process everything. I need to plan for Milo tomorrow. I need to iron the shirts for next week. I need to sleep and make something lovely and get back in touch with something good – be in the garden, or stroke Viking, or paint.

Val tossed and turned in bed. Another sleepless night. She sat up suddenly, Viking, her cat, leaping up and scuttling away. He turned and looked at her as he left the room. Val pushed back the duvet. It was hot, or she was hot, she wasn't sure which, and dawn was already breaking. Val rubbed her chest; the ache there wouldn't go away. Occasionally, she felt herself gasp or cough.

Her heat subsided and she found herself shivering. She didn't want to lie down again though, so she pulled the duvet around her and leant her back against the bed's headboard.

It hadn't made sense to her, Brenda going on about the red kites, but at the same time it had. Val felt the thud her chest again and she coughed. It felt as though she had been squeezed, much like one of the squeaky animals she used for the MIMs. She did feel a bit like that – used and wrung out.

It was no good. She'd have to get up even though her clock said it was five in the morning. So much to do.

In the kitchen, she made herself a cup of tea and gave Viking an early morning breakfast. She sat watching him and longed for his capacity to make everything expansive and spacious. His eating was an act of wholeheartedness. When he had finished, he licked his lips and looked at her with an open face and clear eyes. He walked to the door, and she felt his communication as clear as could be – no doubts, no confusion. She let him out into the morning and heard the early birds warn each other of his presence.

No doubts, no confusion. That would be wonderful. What, she wondered, did she really want, for herself, for Milo, for Joe? Just to be sure? Secure? She knew the feel; it was the feel Viking had just given her: no doubts, no confusion.

Getting up that early meant she was tired before she even started her working day. Louise had left a message asking for an update on how the work was going, whether Mel and Simon were ready to put in for the adoption order. Val had intended to phone Louise back, but the day had ended before she'd found the time. The session with Joe had worn her out, and then the supervision with Brenda – well, that was just confusing!

She put the video camera on to charge. She got out her planning sheet for the previous session with Milo, intending to review the plan. Her goals, she saw, were to help him increase his eye contact with Mel, to relax as Mel checked for any hurts, and to be able to stop and start in a game of motorboat, motorboat helped by Mel and herself. Well, none of that had worked. She just remembered her feeling of rage at his rejection of her loving attention to the planning of the session and the organisation of her bag. She remembered his distance from them, literal and figurative, as he had run across the hall to the room after she and Mel had collected him from class. Her head felt full. She shook it slightly, trying to dislodge the sensation of porridge that filled her, suffocating her thinking as well as her feeling. Maybe looking at the video may provide an idea of what she needed to plan.

She brought up the video on her laptop. The voices seemed echoey and metallic. Her voice sounded strained and a bit too high pitched. "Breath woman!" she said to herself, and that irritating cough happened again.

She remembered the dream she'd had about Milo being a fish, vulnerable and terrifying, flitting from one to the other. Too slippery to get hold of. She got up from her desk and wandered over to her bookshelf, her index finger running over the spines of her books, the sound of her voice still irritating and tinny in her ears even though she couldn't bear to watch the video anymore.

Fish. Jung. Theraplay and Jung? Now that was a connection she hadn't made before. Why fish? She picked up "The Red Book". Jung said that the battle with the sea monster was the attempt to free ego-consciousness from the grip of the unconscious. Jung said that the fish was used for the god who became man.

Val smiled. Milo? God? Well, he maybe thought he was a god and wanted to have utter and unending power over the whole world. And his unconscious? Did he have one? All the literature would say that he did, but it seemed as if all the literature she was being drawn to was about grown-ups, not the Milos or Joes of this world. Neither of them, she thought, ever had the luxury of time to even start to get a sense of themselves as people before they had to learn to just survive. To hold their souls together with nothing more than the very skin that surrounded them. She thought about the sores and cigarette burns that had been found on Joe when he went to his first foster carers. It seemed that even his skin boundary had been pierced by his early care.

They had had no time, and now she felt like she had no time to catch them: Joe with his too fast wagging puppyishness and Milo with his too vulnerable scary slippery fishiness.

It was the lack of time that left her breathless, she suddenly realised. It wouldn't take long to phone the social worker; Louise didn't want lots of processing and words. She wanted headlines – the work was going well, another eight more sessions, Mel was practising the activities at home, all is good. That was enough of the story for her. And, on the surface, that was exactly it. Milo didn't wet the bed anymore; he did as Mel told him to. Mel and Simon wanted him to be their son, so they wanted the adoption to be finalised. And yet, yet, the fire had sunk deep into Milo, to a place Val couldn't reach. He wasn't even battling the sea monster. Like the picture in "The Red Book", the barge sailed on, not oblivious but not engaging with the sea monster that lurked beneath the waves.

It was a farce and a stalemate that everyone held their breath around, not wanting to rock the boat in case the monster overwhelmed them all. But seeing that meant Val could breathe again. She wasn't sure if she could tell anyone that. Brenda, yes, she would get it, but the actual circle of adults in

Milo's life? Would anyone hear how the thread had been broken, and that he needed time and time and more time to repair the rupture? Who wanted to hear that?

She longed to make Milo's life better, whatever that may mean, and help him live life to his full potential. She'd helped him to be obedient, but the pain in his soul had just been driven in like a nail so deep in the wood that it could no longer be retrieved, unless the wood was sanded gently away over time. His personal "living his life to the full" was so very different to what the adults wanted and hoped for him when he was removed from his birth family and placed with Mel and Simon.

Val shook her head and went back to her desk. She watched the frantic actions of herself and Mel wanting to engage Milo. The look in his eyes in the video made her cry. She had done that to him by tearing off his only defence: his intact psychic skin. Too much, too quickly. Resistance hadn't been fertile for him; it had been poison. She would have to live with that and find some way to forgive herself. She hadn't given him her time; she had been too worried about the grown-ups wanting him fixed and too caught up in seeing such hopes in the MIM.

Grace met with Val to talk about how the work was going. Usually Val just wrote a report once a term, but Grace seemed particularly interested in the process and had asked to meet to talk about how things were progressing. Val invited her to The Cottage, made her a cup of tea and invited her to sit down on the sofa in the lounge. Grace settled, folding her leg underneath her, reminding Val of the way Viking settled himself in a sunny spot.

"I thought this was meant to be Theraplay?" Grace asked. "Why isn't the foster carer involved?"

Val was still stinging from the breakdown of the connection with Milo and was therefore defensive in her reply. "Joe just isn't ready for that yet. If he gets too close to Nickie at the moment, then he'll be frightened off. We've got to take it step by step."

Val thought she could see the suspicion on Grace's face. She was unsure herself and couldn't really be clear if what she was doing with Joe was a reaction against the awfulness of what had happened with Milo — if that could even be called awful as everyone was saying how much better he was. It just felt right to work with Joe on his own. She was showing his foster carer the video of the session and thinking with her about what that meant for home, how she could use some of the activities to fine-tune her care, learning what the signs of resistance were and how to respond to them. And it meant that Val was getting the raging and hatred directed at her without it having a fallout on Nickie. Realistically, Val knew she was disposable in the relationship. Nickie wasn't.

"So," Grace continued, "explain to me why this is helping Joe."

Val felt herself bristling, still oversensitive, but caught it within herself. She made herself look at Grace, hearing in her head Brenda saying, "People are people; what you do with clients you do with everyone else. You don't do Theraplay, you are Theraplay." Grace's face was open, her eyes soft and curious. Her direct tone had just caught Val on the hop, raw as she was from the challenges of the work with Milo and Joe. It seemed to Val that Grace really wanted to know what this work was about.

Val didn't want to be tongue-tied but she was. She was so passionate about Theraplay and working with children and families that sometimes if felt like a burning in her solar plexus – either that or she was getting heartburn.

"It is so hard to explain," she said, thinking that sounded pathetic. "Do you have children, Grace?"

Grace's face melted again and her smile answered Val's question more eloquently than words ever could. "A little girl."

"What was it like when you looked at your daughter's face for the first time?"

"Rapture." Grace came out with the word without hesitation or any sense of withholding her heartfeltness of her love for her child.

"I couldn't stop looking at her. I wanted to understand every move and sound. We fell in love immediately."

"I want that for Joe. Does that sound crazy coming from a professional? I want to make it possible for him to fall in love with a grown-up. I really want it to be Nickie, but…"

Grace uncurled her leg from under her and leant forward. "My baby had to let me look after her. She was totally helpless." Grace's eyes were shining. Val could see that she was feeling the significance of what was being spoken about. "That must be utterly terrifying for Joe! To be helpless."

"Why would he trust a grown-up? What earthly use are they to him when they hit and hurt and drop him as if he's nothing? Sometimes I just feel an edge of the humiliation he might feel. It is what I imagine an ice burn must be like – it hurts, then it's numb until it really, really hurts and you just can't bear it."

Val shook her head at her attempt to imagine what it might be like in Joe's inner world.

"I don't want to hurt him, but I don't want him to feel he has to be in charge all the time to stop the hurts, so I have to push him. I have to believe that he wants to connect, somewhere deep down, maybe really hidden and skewed, but there is still the same thirst to be loved that your daughter had. You danced with her to learn her sounds and the meaning of her moves. I have to work out Joe's dance and not be seduced by it."

Val looked anxiously at Grace. She didn't usually talk about her work in this way; it was too woolly and fluffy for most people. Most professionals who commissioned her work wanted clear outcomes and goals set at the start of the intervention. Saying "I just want him to fall in love" didn't fall into the category of acceptable professional discourse.

"So how do you do that?" Grace really wanted to know.

"The same way you did with your daughter – just adapted to make sure I don't scare him off by getting too close too soon because of his trauma. I want to play all those games that you played with your child: peek-a-boo, this little piggy, whatever. The game doesn't really matter. I want him to know that I really think he is the best, the loveliest little boy in the whole wide world and the only person in my head. Of course, I use a lot of theory to explain what I do – Allan Schore, Bruce Perry – have you read his *The Boy Who Was Raised as a Dog?*"

Grace shook her head.

"You should, it's really readable." Val caught herself. She was on a roll; she could easily gabble on about the theory for hours.

"But the theory isn't the heart of it," she said aloud, talking to herself as much as Grace. "Theory keeps me safe; it is my structure; it is how I explain what I do and why I do it. But the explanations come after – after I have been in there with the child and been so tuned into them that I know what they need and how much they can take."

"What if you get it wrong?"

Val shuddered, the shame rising like a red tide on her neck as Milo came to her mind.

"You try and make it right."

She knew most children are "forgiving and resilient", but Milo was neither. His resilience and forgiveness had been annihilated by his first experiences of being helpless in the face of those who were there to take care of him. Would she ever be able to make it right for him?

Grace looked at Val's stricken face and realised in that moment the cost of the work that Val did. There was nothing to say. They sat together in the room in The Cottage made to feel like a lounge but which was a professional space, silent; wordlessly knowing what couldn't be shared and understood because the words themselves took them away from the knowing.

After the conversation with Grace, Val thought she was being too cautious about her work with Joe. It was time for Nickie to be involved.

Joe looked up at Val, and she found her heart breaking. What was it about the way he looked at her? It was as if his face said he hadn't been fed for weeks, an old message that still crept through. In her stomach, she knew what it must have been like for him, that piercing need to just get something in his mouth and into his stomach. How did she know, could she know? Once it reached her mind and awareness, she started to doubt herself; and as the word questions came into her head, she saw the light go out in Joe's eyes. That moment of meeting had just gone by. She stored it away, puzzled at the meaning of that hot and intense moment. Joe looked as he always did, the wagging-tailed puppy, and underneath that she could sense the unyielding rock-like defence.

Good stuff is taken away, bad stuff happens and everyone carries on as normal. It was her mantra about the impact of trauma – something that helped her to think about what to do next. Her list of Theraplay activities said that there were three more games before she would carry out the feeding activity with Joe. But she felt that good stuff had been taken away, so carrying on as normal didn't seem a fruitful option to her.

"Joe," she said, "I had a sudden thought that you might be hungry. Why don't you sit here?" She pushed a cushion into the corner of the room and made it into a cosy spot for him. "Nickie," she said to his carer, "you come here," and pointed to a cushion next to Joe.

Nickie glared at her. This wasn't what Val said they would be doing. One minute she was saying you need structure to stay safe, and now she was changing the activities around!

"It's OK," Val said, picking up on the narrowing of Nickie's eyes and the stiffness in her abdomen. "I just have a feeling that right at this moment Joe needs some food. I think there may have been lots of times when he didn't have food right when he needed it, when he was a very little boy, before you started to look after him. I don't know if he believes that food will always be there for him. I wonder if that's why he keeps coming down in the night to see what he might be able to find just in case."

Joe gave no sign of listening to the conversation. He sat in the corner, and it was as if there was a Perspex wall between him and Nickie.

Val shook her head inwardly. Nickie seemed cut up and hurt by what she saw as Joe's betrayal in taking food from the kitchen at night, so today it just seemed counterproductive to ask her to offer Joe nurture. Now Nickie was involved in the work, Val didn't want to be the person most attuned to Joe's needs. She just gave him a packet of chocolate buttons. While he ate, she sang gently, the words not really mattering but at the same time really mattering, all put to the tune of 'My Bonnie Lies over the Ocean'. It didn't quite scan, but that didn't matter.

"Joe has food to eat,
he'll always have food to eat,
he's happy with his food to eat,
good old Joe.
He eats it, slowly,

he eats it very fast.
Always food,
it tells him that he is loved."

Joe ate the buttons rapidly and just let the empty packet fall. He curled in on himself and pulled a blanket over his head, almost as if he was hiding from the world. It was hard to imagine that he could be comfortable with his body tied in a knot like that. Val thought about the way very small children thought that they couldn't be seen if they couldn't see. He was like an infant.

"Where's Joe gone?" she asked gently in motherese. She reached out and stroked his back under the blanket. "There he is!" The silence was massive. It was as if he was holding his breath.

"Joe, I won't hit you," she found herself saying. *But*, she thought, *Nickie is emotionally hitting you today. Poor Nickie, this is such a tough time for her.* Val knew she felt guilty about the times her compassion ran out in the face of Joe's persistent difficulty in complying. She was in need of as much nurture as Joe, maybe more, as she was aware of just how much was lost by not being able to stay in relationship with him.

"Nickie, you just gently touch Joe's back here. See, you can feel his spine and his ribs, and Joe can feel the warmth of your hand," Val said, taking her hand and placing it on Joe's back. She kept her hand in contact with Nickie's, supporting her.

With the touch, Nickie couldn't stay angry with Joe. She ached inside daily with the injury she saw in Joe and how it came out in ways that just made his life harder than it needed to be, and he couldn't see what he was missing out on. Little by little, Nickie and Joe were letting each other in.

CHAPTER EIGHT

Middle Phases

Val always tried to arrive early for sessions with children. From experience, she knew that you could never be sure what you would find at school. Today was one of those days. A delivery of new textbooks had been stored in the room that Val usually used. She was used to having to move the table and chairs to make space for the session, but the extra boxes made the space seem even smaller. She covered them over with the blanket she usually put on the floor. It might unsettle Joe a bit not having the familiarity of the blanket there but, on balance, Val thought it would be more useful to have the boxes of books covered because Joe would want to investigate them.

She tried the video camera in various places to get as much coverage of the room as possible but, even so, there would be blind spots. It would be so much easier to do this work at The Cottage with video cameras set up and a good way of recording sound, but then, this was about what was best for Joe. The probability was that if Nickie had to bring him to sessions each week, Joe would miss sessions if she was at work or on training, and they would all have the anxiety about him bolting again. Without coming into school, she would miss out on those corridor conversations, not just about Joe, but about the other Joe-like children in the school. It would have been harder for her to support school staff too; they received a lot of Joe's distress. She always hoped that what she did spread a little beyond the one child she was in school to work with. The other Jo still haunted her. She hadn't caught sight of her again.

The smile on her face was somewhat constructed; she had to cognitively remind herself of the positives. She held on to the idea that if she positively reframed the hard labour of book and furniture removal, travel to school and the unpredictability of rooms, that in the end she would be able to stay in her warm and welcoming state. There was nothing forced, however, when she went to the class to fetch Joe. He was always a pleasure to see, at least for her. She wasn't quite sure why he'd made her smile from the start. Despite his swearing and his spitting and his kicking, his face was open and what you saw was what you got.

Joe wanted to be carried to the room – thankfully, he was still small for a six-year-old. Whether this was the legacy of neglect or whether his parents were just small, no one seemed to quite know; he certainly ate enough now. In fact, he often couldn't stop eating, would go away and throw up, and then come back and start again. He had raged at Nickie for days when she put limits on his eating, swearing she was starving him and depriving him of food. Such was the vehemence of his argument that his school had called Grace, thinking it was a safeguarding issue. It could have so easily broken the placement when it had barely begun, but Grace saw a repeating pattern and that was the end of the matter. Joe was told that it was up to Nickie to take care of him and she was the best person to decide what was the right amount for him to eat.

In the Theraplay, they had found all kinds of ways to help Joe realise that food came with a person attached and that the pleasure of being held while being fed and the relaxation of someone knowing your needs was the nurture he needed. Usually, now he didn't need to find the snack as the very first activity; he had some confidence that he would always have the snack at the end of the session.

The questions started from the moment Val picked up Joe from class. Normally, she and Nickie did this together.

"Where is Nickie?"

Val explained that to be the best carer she could, every year Nickie had to do training and today she'd had to go to one of those training courses. Val knew Nickie had explained this to Joe. They had discussed the best way to put it, knowing that he would need the same form of words from both Nickie and Val to make it sound real.

"Do you mean she's at school, too?" Joe asked.

"That's right," Val agreed. This confirmed to her that Nickie had told him; that was the way they'd agreed she would put it to him.

"Will I still get a snack?"

"Yes, of course," said Val, making a mental note that feeding might have to be the first activity of the session, rather than the last as she had planned.

She was pleased she'd turned on the video camera before fetching Joe, as he kicked out at her as soon as they were in the room. She put him down onto his feet and knelt in front of him.

"Joe, do you remember our rules? No hurts, have fun, stick together?"

But Joe wasn't listening. The different order of the room, the absence of Nickie and whatever else might be going on inside him was all too much. He lunged at Val. If she hadn't dodged to the side, he would have headbutted her. As it was, she couldn't hold onto him; and he bolted under the table. She actually felt pleased. He could have made it out through the door. She had spent most of an early session trying to find out where in the school he had run to – so it seemed to her that he did at some level want to stay close to her, a minuscule and minute nod to attachment, but something to hold onto.

She waited quietly, humming to herself. He didn't emerge.

"I think it might have been a bit scary coming without Nickie and finding the room all different with boxes and stuff," she said to the thin air. "Poor Joe must wonder what we are going to do. I think I'll read out my list." She kept her voice even and melodic, not making any effort to approach Joe or make eye contact.

If he was spooked by the changes, then he needed her presence and her voice to help him sooth himself.

"Come into the room – check," she sang. "Check out Joe? Check!"

Did she imagine that she heard him stiffen at this?

"Well, I know some things are a bit different today because you don't usually hide, so my check-up says Joe has some big feelings. Next game, hide-and-seek! I think you knew what we were going to do! You are so smart! I'm coming to find Joe!"

She made a big show of looking in places where he just couldn't be hidden – on the shelves, underneath her bag. And so the session continued. Val slowly enticing Joe out and into relationship. In minutes, the session only lasted 15. In timescales of healing – immeasurable, exhausting. As Val carried Joe back to the classroom, he rested his head on her shoulder drumming his hands on her back in time to her paces.

Val felt drained. The session had only been 15 minutes, and Joe was 90 centimetres tall, and how many kilos, 15? He certainly was very small for his age. But she felt like she had just done 10 rounds with a heavyweight.

She slumped into a chair in the school staffroom, too weary even to make herself a cup of tea. She needed to shut her eyes but when she did, it was as if the session replayed itself behind her eyelids in colourful detail. "First catch your child", came to mind. What was she doing, making rabbit pie from scratch? She certainly felt like she was making a social child from scratch, and she wasn't sure whose idea was stronger of what the world should be like – her's or Joe's.

When she opened her eyes, there was a cup of tea on the table in front of her. Mrs Potter's back was just going out through the door. Val smiled.

"Thanks," she said.

Mrs Potter turned back and smiled. Val was shocked at the normalness of how easy caring was and how lovely it felt. Tears came and she was pleased that the moment of meeting with Mrs Potter was brief. She didn't think at this moment in time she could explain why that touch of compassion and connection from a colleague was so overwhelming. She had just spent 15 minutes in a very individual and unique hell. A hell that, to Joe, felt a familiar place – a place, to him, of play.

Brenda was still acutely aware of Val's vulnerability at present. Frankly, she was worried about her fitness to practice. These two boys she was seeing, something about the work with them had triggered a deep crisis of identity in Val. Brenda had encouraged Val to come for additional supervision. Brenda wanted to support Val to find her feet again. She picked up from where they had left off the last time Val had been so distressed.

They talked about the school session with Joe and the resistance he had shown, how it seemed that he was ready for Val to push his window of tolerance a bit, give him more opportunities to experience relationship with both herself and Nickie. They talked about Milo. It took all of Val's courage to talk openly about how she felt she had damaged Milo by being too keen to engage with him and retriggering his trauma. Brenda felt, however, that Val was holding back, not getting to the core of her own resistance in her work.

"What don't you know?" Brenda found herself asking. What a stupid question, she thought to herself, if either of us knew, we wouldn't be here struggling with this painful stuckness.

As expected, Val answered, "If only I knew that, things would be OK."

As she said it, Val shifted in her chair as if something, just some small thing, had moved. Her breath deepened. Brenda saw the movement and thought she needed to just keep speaking, not knowing what to say and not following the usual pattern of her supervision practice.

"Sometimes it's like one person carries all the burdens of a time. They come up with an idea or plan that takes off, and soon it isn't just one person's idea. It takes on a life of its own. It might even spring up in more than one place at a time, like people have been thinking along the same lines and suddenly all that thinking comes together and there is understanding of something."

She looked at Val. This didn't feel like it was going well, but at least they were lost in it together. She felt as though she was talking as a soothing mother: calming a child not by what she said but by the way she said it.

"What is happening inside you as I talk, Val?"

"You have no idea, do you? You have no idea what it's like to be with Milo and to be so wrong-footed all the time. I don't know how he does it to me. I go in ready to be open and kind, yet it sours as soon as I'm in his presence. I can understand why his mum wants to give up. I find I can't think about anything with him, or near him, or after him. He suffocates me. I…" She stopped herself.

Brenda was convinced she was going to say that she hated him, but neither could voice that.

"How can I do any good in this?" Val asked. "I don't feel able to make any difference to him, so why am I doing this work in the first place?"

"I don't know," Brenda said, "it's just that sometimes it seems like the universe gives you the experiences you need to make sense of things for yourself if you can stick with the not knowing long enough."

"Are you saying that I am using these children for my own benefit?" Val could feel her face starting to go red and her chest become tight. Her throat had seized up.

"No! No! It's not as straightforward as that!" Brenda was catching the tension, feeling defensive in response to Val's defensiveness. This oversensitivity was taking on a life of its own. "It's just that it's complicated and we don't always know what is our unconscious injury and what comes from the people we are working with. Sometimes you just have to trust your goodness. Sometimes you just can't know."

"And you call yourself a fucking supervisor! You take my money and you sit there and you tell me you don't know!"

For a moment they both sat there, both shocked at Val's outburst. Then Val grabbed her bag and coat and rushed from the room.

"Val! Let's talk about this." But it was too late. Val had gone. Brenda debated whether to go after her. Was she safe?

She was a supervisee not a client. She heard Val's car start up and stall. She looked out of the window and saw Val take a deep breath and steady herself physically as she sat behind the wheel. The car restarted and pulled away safely. She is a supervisee, Brenda thought. She is a good, solid therapist. She will process it. I will wait for her to contact me or wait until our next planned session. But Val's words stung. It was always core, deep questions she had, maybe every therapist had. Are we good enough? Are we doing this for the best of motivations? Are we getting off on the suffering of others? What does caring about really mean?

Val was consumed by shame as she drove away. She had to consciously and physically work at driving safely. Thankfully, she had no more children to see that day. She went home – another huge advantage of working for herself. Viking was there to greet her; he knew she was upset and didn't care. He just wanted his needs met and after she had fed him, he sat beside her while she stared into space, stroking him. Listening to his purring, looking out onto the green of the garden and being mesmerised by the movement of the wind on the leaves.

It was in the shower that it came to Brenda. She wasn't even thinking about Val at that point. She'd done her yoga and gone for a walk. She'd made a note to herself that they needed more milk, and Edward said he'd get it on the way back from the timber merchants. He'd left early, so she was in the house on her own. With no clients until mid-morning, she had been able to take her time over a cup of tea before taking a shower.

Val was thinking of herself as a victim.

Brenda felt it with a conviction, although she hadn't even realised she'd been puzzling over it. Maybe she hadn't. Maybe it had just been bubbling away beneath the surface. She was suspicious of the conviction, questioning it. Why did she think that? Where had that idea come from? She rubbed her hair dry vigorously. It would be so much easier if she could rub that idea out of her head too. Thinking of Val as a victim didn't sit comfortably but the more she thought about it, the more the idea stood up to her scrutiny: the unexpected flare-up when she had tried to challenge Val, the sense of Val being overwhelmed by things that in the past she had managed with flair and creativity, the flipping from anger to tears. It was secondary trauma.

How was she going to talk with Val about this?

Milo kicked his heels – not metaphorically, but literally. Sitting on the chair in the school reception, his lower legs swung forwards and then back so far that the heels banged the bottom of the chair. He could see the receptionist working hard not to get irritated. He could see that she knew he was the "poor adopted boy" who had had "a rough start" and he would have been sent to see the Head if this therapist wasn't coming in today. The swing-tap, swing-tap continued at a regular pace. She actually found that if she went with it, it was kind of soothing. She could almost fit words to it. It made her think of her daughter when she was young: "This is the way we swing our legs" she could almost hear. Well, really, she could hear in her head. It brought a smile to her face to remember her daughter, concentrating with a pencil in her hand, trying to draw.

Crash!

Milo had swung his legs so hard that his feet had caught the edge of the coffee table and the magazines and school newsletters for visitors to look at were strewn across the floor. It was a rude awakening from her reverie of the lovely time with her own child. She didn't know how to respond; her emotions swung again. Irritation to cuteness, to irritation to cuteness. What was she meant to feel about him? He was just giving her a look, a hard stare.

Paddington Bear. She couldn't help it – just imagine him in a duffle coat and red hat. Please look after this bear. She got up with a smile on her face and was about to speak – she probably would have offered him a marmalade sandwich and said to be careful about putting his sticky paws on the magazines.

As she moved towards him, lifting the counter of the office desk so she could get to him, she noticed his smile. *It isn't shy*, she thought. She hadn't even registered that is how she judged his demeanour. His face looks wide-eyed and open, like an infant, she thought. He really was a lost little bear from darkest Peru, and her heart missed a beat for him.

In harmony, they bent down to pick up the magazines; but just at that moment, the door to the Head's office opened and Milo stiffened. He sat back on the chair, back to swinging his legs, back to a hard-faced stare that left her feeling as if the rug had been pulled out from under her feet. Back to irritation towards him.

She picked up the magazines herself not asking him for help, not expecting anything. It just felt uncomfortable, and she was pleased when his therapist arrived. She pushed the visitors' book towards her saying nothing and experienced a sense of relief when Milo followed the woman through the corridor. That was weird, she thought. It was as if she had been pushed around. She sat down to the computer but couldn't for the life of her remember what she was doing. It was as though her brain had been wiped. She was just left feeling empty and lost and a bit baffled, as if she'd been sucked into something and then spat out and not really knowing if she wanted to be in or out.

The bell rang for break and the sounds of children – voices and feet – seeped through the cloud that had enveloped her. Someone put a cup of tea on her desk. She picked it up, feeling the steam rise and condense on her face. It was as if she needed that to thaw her and bring her back to moment.

"Miss, Miss, Angus is bleeding!" pleaded a small, insistent voice.

Indeed, Angus was bleeding from a skinned knee and tears were bravely being held at bay. She was back to the moment. Mental treacle waded through so she could help Angus by sponging down his knee and letting him sit there for the rest of break with a damp hand towel held against the graze.

When the bell went for the end of break, Angus said, "Thanks, Miss," and headed back to class.

Shadows and ghosts still sat on the chairs – the dark and brooding form of Milo, Angus, feathery, grey, lively and dispersing. Milo's presence sat like a clammy brick, she thought. You couldn't put him out of your mind even though you really, really wanted to. The feel of it sullied the open need

Angus had to be cared for when he was hurt and his wholehearted and grateful expectations of her care for him.

Joe hated it when he was put to bed, alone in his room. The night light was left on for him, but he wished it wasn't. He could half see things, and he didn't want to think about what they might be. He didn't know what to make of this low level of stimulation. He wanted to shut down, or open up – it didn't really matter which. But this in the middle stage was just unbearable. He got out of bed and jumped up and down. He knew the sound of his jumping would bring his foster carer back to the room and he would get told off. What a relief! He did still exist, and she did still exist, and the world did still exist.

"Joe, go to bed."

He knew the first time she would always be calm and understanding but the seventh or eighth time, then he could get her to be cross and then she would turn off the light, in anger, and then he could be in oblivion. She sometimes asked, "What would help you sleep?" But he didn't know. That just made it worse. It was like a prickly seed between him and his pyjamas, irritating away, just a bit at first until he had to take off all his clothes and run to the shower. His social worker came to visit after that one. She said he would have to think about his behaviour.

I do, he thought to himself. I do think. It just didn't make any sense to him. He thought, but it seemed he wasn't thinking in the way they wanted him to think. If he thought the way he wanted him to think, it felt too weird and out of control. He was wrong, it seemed, whatever he did.

Val wondered what would happen if she could video Joe and Milo outside of sessions. She was particularly interested in what they did when they were on their own. But how could good-minded professionals intrude on the children's privacy in their own rooms? It seemed unethical. What would it be like to be watched at all times?

Val thought about herself. She felt watched at all times. She watched herself feeling watched at all times. Layer upon layer of trying to second-guess what she should be doing. So many unseen expectations to please that she couldn't keep up, and they led to her feeling disconnected from herself. Like she was looking at herself moving and talking but it didn't quite feel real. She could feel lost and totally unsure of who she was once she was on her own. There was a deep connection between her and the children she worked with in that way. It made her uncomfortable. Whose benefit was she working for? That is why Brenda's question had stung so much; she asked it of herself all the time and didn't trust her own beneficence.

Was it OK that she got to understand herself in the work, just as much as the children got to understand themselves? But she wasn't even certain that the children understood themselves any better by the end of the work. In those quiet moments when she wasn't frantically busy with calls and notes and crises, those times when she sat and contemplated, the big questions were posed: *What was she doing? What was the point of it all?*

Have a cup of tea. Have a biscuit. Think about the training session that needs to be prepared. Think about how you haven't washed the car and what people might think if you turn up for meetings in a muddy vehicle. Anything, really, to "do" rather than "be". The hurting in Milo's expression came back to her mind. The mismatch in yearnings between him and Mel. The horror of I don't know; the fear of what will come up if she stayed with "not knowing" for her, for Milo, for Joe.

Yes, she would so like to have a camera in Milo's room at night to work out what was really going on with his bed-wetting. There were so many speculations. Mel thought he was getting back at her. Louise thought he was too scared to get out of bed. Maybe Val thought he might be scared of now or maybe scared by memories of the past. Or maybe fear was just a habit. Maybe it was about a familiar smell: the report said that the house smelt strongly of urine when Milo was removed. Maybe he just didn't realise he needed to go. Maybe he shut down at night completely to blot out the painful arousal inside so he didn't feel the need to wee. Maybe letting go just felt nice, a release of tension, like an orgasm.

Val found all the possibilities fascinating. It was like a choppy sea of potential feelings. More than a choppy sea – more like the boiling waters of a rip tide. It felt dangerous to go there to try and work it all out, and it also felt enlivening to Val that "she was the only one" who could or would go into that dangerous place.

But she didn't want it to feel good; that felt ghoulish. She felt in a choppy place herself – pride and disgust at her professional interest. She felt both doubt and certainty about what she was doing, and that was a tension she wanted to end. Not knowing for certain was wearing her out. Not being able to say "it is this" or "do this and it will be fine" or "it is because this happened to him" was distressing because the adults who loved and cared about these boys wanted to know what to do to give them peace. It would give her such peace to be certain, just for once. It was like a plea. Just let me know what to do to make it better for Milo and Joe! But what did it mean, make it better? Stop the hurt. Just stop the hurt. It is too much to bear.

The drive to Brenda's was always soothing. Living out in the countryside meant that there was always a time for reflection and a routine to the approach. Val knew that Brenda would want to start from where they had finished last time; together, they would have to talk about Val's outburst and find meaning in it.

Val knew Brenda would have spoken to her consultant, another woman. Val smiled, she felt that the wisdom of their practice was shared and transmitted like a passing on of sacred experiences; although, she also felt uncomfortable that yet again a religious or spiritual aspect had somehow sneaked into her thinking about her Theraplay cases. She, who was a committed non-believer.

She had been pleased when her brother, in his retirement, traced their family tree and declared a connection to Vikings on the maternal line. That was why she had called her cat Viking. Sometimes she thought she might take one of those DNA tests that claimed to tell you your ancestry, but then she'd think, what if it told me I was just a bog-standard English person? What would it matter anyway where she came from? What this thinking told her was something about how she wanted to see herself, where she wanted to feel at home. I want to belong somewhere kind, Val thought. I want to like me; not think of myself in the way my upbringing made me evaluate myself.

Did that mean she should stop doing this kind of work? Or maybe she should find a husband. Or become a man? It wasn't about actually belonging somewhere kind. It was about being kind.

Sometimes the fantasy of what "might be" was easier than facing the reality of the here and now. Gee, she was good at judging herself in a negative light, supported by a cultural system that saw caring professions, and the women who offer the care, as of little and dubious value. She wanted to be a Viking warrioress. She wanted to be a person – not a white, middle-class, Judaeo-Christian woman, do-gooder, know-it-all who could be found out any moment as a crap woman who had no child of her own.

Professionally, it had taken a lot to accept that she carried her prejudices, like when Grace surprised her about growing up on a farm. It had been hard not to drown in her feeling of shame but to accept that this was a useful and non-judgemental reminder that there were more things to know about herself and the world than she'd yet had chance to learn. Today would be a time to learn, and not to be consumed by the shame she was feeling. Although it was taking a lot of courage and self-talk to see it that way.

Did she really do this job to save herself? The reality of her long-standing relationship with Brenda and the regularity of the routine of going for supervision made it possible to face the task of asking herself that question.

"How can I do any good in this?" Val asked. "I don't feel able to make any difference to Milo or Joe, so why am I doing this work in the first place?"

"Because you are. The doing of it is important, not because of what you are doing, but because you are being there," Brenda replied.

In exploring the conundrum, they made a sort of poem together.

"I am angry, I am so angry."

"Who with?"

"With me, with me. I am no different to Milo."

"How are you like Milo?"

"I can't feel. I can't connect. I hate and I tremble and I pour my shit out onto the other."

"Be Milo."

"I'd punch you, and I'd be scared that I could do that and I'd run away. Joe wants to curl up in your lap like a kitten with a lost mummy. Milo…"

It was like being pulled up into the sky with the kites and then being left to fall. Feeling powerful and at the same time exposed and vulnerable. It was about being without a mother. Being without the dance of connection. The comfort of being me because of nothing more, yet the everything of a net of closeness, and being held, and fed, and feeling certainty like warmth. Without that bedrock of connection, it was like falling and falling into nowhere and being nothing and no one, forever. Eternity of nothing. Dreadful.

Brenda couldn't see into Val's head, but she could see her eyes move and her breath change. She was close to the core of the distress, where the anguished cry of "I need my mummy" was. Where there is a knowing that no one will come and the reality of utter, utter abandonment and nothingness. The wound was all-consuming and intense and naked. And they were just sitting there together, two women, making meaning and making connection. It was exhausting. It was exhilarating. It was mothering. Being kind, wise and strong in the face of "everything".

Val gave a huge sigh. *From the brink*, she thought. *I am back from the brink. I've faced the most awful and discovered I am me.*

I don't know how to say what we have done, Brenda thought. *We have done something. We have made something beautiful in our togetherness.*

I have to just be there, Val knew.

The dance between Val and Brenda was such that it was as if they didn't know who was talking, or even if there was talking.

CHAPTER NINE

Endings

Still working out what had happened in supervision and feeling far more comfortable and grounded, Val found herself looking forward to continuing the work with Joe and knew she needed to speak with Mel and Simon about what was next in the work with Milo.

She arrived at Joe's school and smiled at the receptionist. After that slightly uncomfortable start on her first visit, she had invested time to talk with Sue at the front desk. She felt that she had become part of the school community, not a central part, but someone who staff knew they could approach. So today she was surprised that Sue didn't smile as Val signed herself in.

The Head had changed just last week. Val was sad to see the previous Head go. She had been a huge support in the work with Joe, giving her staff tacit approval to take time to speak with Val about the impact Joe had on them personally and on his class. It had been an unpleasant leaving for the Head: the last inspection suggested the school "needed improvement" because of its SATS results and lack of documentation. So, many parents and staff felt bemused that the culture of kindness hadn't been seen as a strength, nor that the level of adversity children came into school with had been taken into account.

Val had sent a welcome email to the new Head and said, when she was settled, that she would welcome the chance to meet with her and explain the work she was doing with Joe. So, it wasn't entirely a surprise when Sue said, "Mrs Shoosmith would like to see you before you see Joe today." But the look on Sue's face made Val's heart beat faster.

Ten minutes later, Val left the Head's office furious. How could one person ruin the work with a child? The Head had unilaterally decided that Val could no longer see Joe in school. More than that, Mrs Shoosmith said that having reviewed Joe's file, she didn't think they could provide the education input he required, so she would be calling a meeting to review his school place.

It had become a fine-tuned sense over the years. Meeting someone for the first time, Val would often have a sense of someone having their own mental health difficulties. When they denied this to themselves, it felt kind of unsafe to Val. She didn't want to intrude on anyone's personal inner world without their agreement, but it made a vital difference to the work she was doing when those around an unsettled child were denying their own struggles. Val felt Mrs Shoosmith didn't like all the awkward feelings that Joe stirred up. Joe made the school messy, so he had to go – at least that is what Val thought was going on. It was hard to challenge when the words that were being used were all about making sure Joe's educational needs were being met in the best way possible.

Val always wanted to approach these things with openness and warmth. Sometimes she wondered if she was just too naive. She wanted to believe that everyone would have the same approach to working together and championing the children who were referred to her. Joe had been one of the easy ones to find so much to enjoy: his energy, his quickness of foot and wit. Yes, he kept them all on their toes and yes, you had to be really on the ball in terms of managing boundaries for him, and yes, you had to have eyes in the back of your head – that was why he had a one-to-one teaching assistant. But at the end of the day, Joe belonged here. This was his community and, in Val's eyes, that community had a more significant role in giving Joe the day in, day out message of belonging than anything she could do in once-a-week therapy. The school and the care Nickie provided were most definitely his lifeline to "normality" of functioning. They were a strong and everyday reminder of how "ordinary everydayness" is what life is about.

The normality of home and school was like a sponge soaking up the complete madness of Joe's early childhood. They couldn't take away the violence and the horror, but they were showing him that they didn't hate him and that they would be a witness when he told them about the violence and horror through the way he behaved. They didn't like what he did and sometimes his peers didn't want to be with him, but tomorrow was another day. Each day they could reset themselves to be loving to him afresh, because they were filled up each night with the security of their own families. Val had been bowled over by the loveliness, compassion and big-heartedness of his classmates. They are bigger, she thought, than this new Head. She was really struggling with the bitterness she was feeling.

Mrs Shoosmith. Even the name left Val feeling irritated. Shoehorn more like, wanting children to be a certain way. Val was both caught up in the indignation and at the same time really curious about where it came from.

Mrs Shoosmith hadn't really looked her in the eye during their 10-minute conversation. The previous week, Mrs Shoosmith had passed her when Val was discussing Joe with the SENDCo. It must have been Mrs Shoosmith's second day in the post. Her mouth had hardened when Sally explained what was happening with Joe and how Val was such a help in thinking through how to manage situations so they could still do the best for Joe while making sure everyone else had their needs met as well. Mrs Shoosmith had just asked Val, "So who pays you? What is your role?" and then just harrumphed when Val explained.

Today's conversation left Val with an unsettled feeling in the pit of her stomach; she'd learnt that that usually meant she was in the presence of someone who was pretty emotionally wobbly. Not that you would see it in Mrs Shoosmith. What was on the surface was clarity. She knew exactly what the school needed to do to improve, and she was not going to let one little boy get in the way of that. It all sounded reasonable, of course, that they weren't the right environment to meet his needs, but it left a bitter taste in Val's mouth because she didn't think that was the reason at all.

Joe saw through people. Val thought that was probably something else she had in common with the children she worked with. She saw through people as well. Maybe not as acutely as Joe, or Milo for that matter, but in some ways she was realising they all came from the same place. The place where, in the unfairness of it all, they ended up feeling it was their fault.

Of course, Joe started to act up even more. Why wouldn't he? He knew he wasn't wanted anymore. The tighter the control became, the more he kicked, literally. He got more sanctions, more exclusions, and that careful and so fragile sense of belonging that had started to grow was brutally (Val thought) torn away from him.

How dare she.

Just going into the school became painful to Val. She felt she needed to be cheery and accessible to the staff when inside she was railing against the unfairness, and her powerlessness to stop Joe being cast out. She sat in the car steeling herself. She knew the work with Joe was not going well anymore because he knew he wasn't wanted in school anymore. They had agreed that she was keep the work in school until the end of term and then next term she would see him in a community venue. She knew by then that he would be permanently excluded. It hadn't been said, but the writing was on the wall.

As she sat there mentally preparing herself, she saw Mrs Shoosmith get out of her own car. She looked like an old woman. It's the body of a street dweller, Val thought. Unbidden, into her mind came a memory of the group of homeless people who lived by the underpass in town. There was one woman there with about four males. Val often stopped to give them some food or hot drinks when it was cold. The woman's eyes never met hers, and Val was left feeling ashamed, as if it were her fault that this woman suffered so much. As if it were her fault that the woman's inner world had collapsed and, with it, her body had collapsed as well. Mrs Shoosmith may be dressed in a business suit. She may have high heels and a briefcase. But seeing her in that vulnerable moment of awkwardness getting out of the car, Val's rage slipped away. She was another person doing what she needed to do to get by in the best way she could.

She would never know the story of Mrs Shoosmith. She may never know the full story of Joe, but Joe wanted her to know something of the story. Even so, it was too painful sometimes for them to sit with it. Sometimes he couldn't. At the moment, Val couldn't. But weirdly they had built up enough of a connection to know they could get back to it, when the time was right. Val thought that Mrs Shoosmith probably hadn't had that experience. She doubted that anyone had tried, or been allowed to try, to know the story, whatever the story was. Maybe Mrs Shoosmith didn't even know herself that her suffering soul could be so visible – so, in her not knowing, she had to eject those that knew, even though she didn't know that she knew that they knew. It was a reflex action. The boy was trouble. The therapist didn't help. Get rid. End of.

Sometimes all you can do is grieve. The work would go on.

She was able to see Joe for one more term before the funding was withdrawn by the multidisciplinary funding panel. They cited the fact that the work had been unsuccessful in maintaining Joe's educational placement.

Unseen by the outside world, or even the world of his family now, Christmas had been a turning point for Milo. The beginning of another end. It was overwhelming. Milo felt like his lungs were filling up with sand, dragging him down until his eyes felt blurry and his head ached. Why? Why did they bring a tree into the house? Why did they put lights all over it? Why were they all happy and noisy?

Mel looked at Milo. She couldn't put her finger on it, but she was aware that something wasn't quite right.

"Milo?" she asked. "Are you OK?"

Milo looked at her and his eyes haunted her. Their black hollowness literally made her flinch. She turned away reaching for another bauble for the tree.

"I'm fine," Milo said, and she was able to convince herself that he was fine.

Inside, Milo felt night and day were fighting it out. Bright lights, tree, dark venomous emptiness. He didn't know what it was, but he still felt like he was drowning. It was so hard to breath. If he let his eyes shut, he could hear the voices in the back of his head: slut, cow. He could hear muffled crashes and a scream. Shouting.

He shook his head trying to get back to the here and now, tinsel and bright lights. Music in the background. Sophie came over to him, curiously, gently wagging a tail and dipping her head to signal playfulness. She pushed her wet nose under his hand. The coldness of nose made him shudder again, shake his head again. Sophie looked up at him, put her paw up to him, and then yelped and fled across the room skidding on the wooden floor to hide behind the sofa as Milo's fist landed on the side of her head.

"Milo!" Mel shouted.

Simon came running into the room. Milo turned and looked at him full in the eye, his face impassive. The voices in his head had shut up; the voices in his head were turning and looking at him with something like admiration.

Simon was bemused. "What happened?"

"He just hit Sophie!" Mel felt her eyes prickle, but she wasn't sure if it was fear or grief or anger.

Simon came right into the room. He put down the tea towel, the drying up forgotten for the moment. "Milo," he asked quizzically, gently, "what happened?"

"She bit me," Milo lied, looking directly into his father's face.

"She's never bitten anyone." Simon frowned and looked over to Mel. "Did you see what happened, Mel?"

"No, I wasn't looking."

"Milo, go to your room," Simon said. "Mum and I need to think about this."

Milo snorted and, without a backward glance, walked out of the room, but he didn't turn left to go up the stairs to his room. Instead, he opened the front door and walked out into the street.

Simon looked at Mel. "Did he just leave?" he asked, disbelieving.

And then they were both running out of the front door.

"Milo! Milo!" Mel shouted as she turned left and Simon turned right.

"I can see him!" Simon shouted and started to run after the small back that was heading up the street to the main road. He was fit and fast and soon caught Milo, grabbing him in his fear and confusion, lifting him into his arms. "Milo, you gave us such a scare," he said, his voice coming out louder and more forcefully than he intended.

Mel ran up to join them sobbing and breathless. "Why did you do that?"

He buried his face in his father's shoulder. They both wanted to believe that was remorse or fear or lesson learnt, but they couldn't see his face to know one way or the other. Milo had now convinced himself that Sophie had bitten him.

They got back to the house, where the front door was still wide open.

Inside, Mel and Simon treated Milo as if he had been injured.

"I'm so sorry I said to go to your room," Simon said, convinced that he had been the cause of Milo's flight. Inside, he was thinking, I must have made him feel like I was rejecting him. I must have reminded him of being shut away in his room when he was with his first family.

They soothed Milo with warmth and food and later tucked him up into bed. Mel sat with him and stroked his head until he fell asleep.

She went downstairs to find Simon in the lounge with Sophie beside him. He was fondling the dog's ears. Her head was on Simon's lap; she looked so miserable. Mel looked at Simon and could see that he was shaken.

"She would never bite!" he said forcefully. "Sophie is incapable of biting even when she's scared. Nothing was happening! Why would he say Sophie bit him?"

Mel went to sit beside him. "I just don't know, Simon. Something wasn't OK for Milo today. When I was putting up the tree, it was like, like he just zoned out. I asked him if he was OK. He said he was, but he looked haggard."

"What, like me now?" Simon said sarcastically.

Mel really looked at her husband and thought, I haven't actually seen you for weeks. He did look haggard. He looked grey, and she hadn't realised that he had lost weight. "What's wrong, Simon?"

"I don't know. It's like, well, like having a ghost or a dangerous snake in the house, but how can I say that about our son? I know he's had a hard start and I want to love him, and I do love him, but sometimes it is like living with a time bomb, and I don't even know what the bomb is about. And then he is lovely, and I have the best time with him, and then I feel like I'm the most rubbish person in the world for thinking such a small child could be a liar and someone who hurts a harmless creature like Sophie." Simon stopped. He couldn't bring himself to look at Mel.

"Sometimes, you know," he whispered, "I wish we had never adopted him. We were OK just the two of us. Now look at us."

He then looked up at Mel and saw her face, frozen in horror at what he was saying. She got up, stiffly, said nothing. She left the room and slammed the door behind her.

Upstairs, Milo heard the door slam. He sighed, relaxed and slept.

Val completed the protocol, all 26 sessions of Theraplay, including spacing out the last sessions and following up with Mel and Simon for several months after she last saw Milo.

She completed her last report and sent it to Louise. Louise replied to her email to say that as the adoption order had been finalised, the case had been passed to the post-adoption support team. No one specific had been allocated, so she had forwarded Val's closing report to the team manager. Val always meant to follow up and make sure that her report was read. She said in it that it was likely Milo would require further therapeutic input in the future and that Mel and Simon should have access to ongoing parental support. She recommended that they were proactively followed up, as she felt they were likely to experience secondary trauma themselves, which may mean it would difficult for them to initiate seeking help. But the joylessness of the final parts of the work was such that she was too happy to lose herself in the new referrals. She never did make that follow-up call.

CHAPTER TEN

Postscript

The meeting with Joe set the direction of Val's research; it reminded her of that very formative time during her therapeutic career and the two boys who had pushed her, personally and professionally, into new depths of engagement with her clients. Until Joe had so unexpectedly got in touch with her, she hadn't realised that she was grateful to them. The original therapeutic work and Joe's contact with her had both helped her focus on her desire to really make sense of the way she worked with children who had been adopted or who were looked after. In terms of her research, documenting those experiences felt like something she could return to the profession before she started to enjoy her retirement.

About six months into her research, she had another text from Joe and she met up with him again. She made the following notes in her research journal.

I got this text from Joe today. "Val, I need to talk to someone. Ever since the baby was born, I have been terrified. I keep dreaming about a cat. I am terrified I am going to kill the baby. I daren't go to sleep. I think I am going mad."

I don't know whether I should tell Joe or not, but it seems to me that he has a right to know what I suspected all those years ago. Even if it wasn't written down anywhere. What he was saying about his dreams suggested to me that he has a memory; it just isn't autobiographical or sequential. I had suspicions at the time but just no facts to hang them on. Joe having dreams about the cat and his fears about harming his baby suggest to me that he may have something imprinted in his body, something that happened before he had enough language to encode the events as a narrative.

This is a transcript from the recording of my meeting with Joe. I recorded it as I was meeting him under the umbrella of research, not as a therapist. I'm writing the transcript here to try and process it myself – research or therapy or just being human? I don't know how to position it at the moment. This is just the sharp end of the conversation. I didn't just leap in as it sounds here.

Val: "Joe, I am going to tell you something that I don't know if it is true or not. It is something I wondered about when I was working with you in the past. There is nothing in the files about this, but I just wondered.

"When you were taken away from home, there had been a spate of cats going missing near where you lived. I was told that the police said they had found a cat on the back doorstep of your house. The story was that it was all wet, but it didn't have a head. There was mess in the kitchen that made the police wonder if the cat had been put in the washing machine. You had glue on your hands and it was on the floor. I think you may have seen a cat's head being pulled off, or something horrible, and I think you may have tried to make it better in whatever way your child self could. I think your mum gave you enough love that you believed things could be made better. I think your mum did the best she could for you but couldn't stop too much horror happening near you."

I was watching Joe really carefully at this point. I wish I had videoed the meeting not just audio recorded it. In my heart and head there were other suspicions that I didn't know whether to voice. I needed to know if I had said enough to ease the trauma memory logjam for him. I've only got my memory to work on, but I remember Joe looking stunned. His mouth opened and his body shuddered. He didn't say anything. He wrapped his arms around himself and he rocked. He went pale. He didn't make eye contact, but then he took a huge, deep breath. He made eye contact with me, the slackness in his cheeks went, he unwrapped his arms. His face flushed and then settled back to a normal colour. He cleared his throat.

What I wasn't going to say to him was the suspicion I always had that it wasn't just about a cat. I had always wondered if Joe's mum had another child, maybe incestuously, and that his grandfather had kept her out of sight so professionals didn't know she was pregnant. If so, I had wondered whether the infant died at birth, or worse. Infanticide is a nasty word. I didn't think he needed me to say that. If the trauma stuckness didn't clear from what I said, I'm sure more would have come up. I think I went into a bit of therapy mode with him. The transcription goes:

Val: "What's happening, Joe? Are you seeing things?"

Joe: "No." (Voice sounds like he might be smiling. A bit of a sigh.)

Joe: "I'm not seeing things. It makes sense. I've had those weird thoughts come into my head all these years, and I thought I must be crazy; but if that happened, that's why I had those thoughts. They weren't me. It was real."

Val: "That was then, Joe. This is now. You can love your baby."

Joe left when he felt a bit calmer. He knew he could contact me again if he needed to and that I would put him in touch with someone he could talk to more.

Throughout the five years of her part-time research, Val wondered about Milo. Ethically, she kept questioning whether she should get in touch with him, or not. She wanted to, but she knew it was about her desire to know how things had turned out, not really about his needs. It had been different with Joe. Joe had initiated the contact.

She knew where Milo was; he had made a good business for himself. He could only have been in his early twenties, but he was running a carpet warehouse and his name often appeared in the local paper usually with the tag line "young up-and-coming businessman" or "young entrepreneur".

It was towards the end of her research that she made the decision to tentatively reach out to Milo. She wrote an old-fashioned letter to his business address, introducing herself and telling him about her research. The invitation was to help her understand from the perspective of children what Theraplay was like and, if he would be happy to talk about his experience all those years ago, to contact her.

Val was surprised when she received a letter back. It wasn't from Milo; it was from his wife. She agreed to meet Val but said it mustn't be part of Val's research and Milo must not know that she had come.

Val made the following record in her research journal.

Transcript of interview with Lucy, wife of Milo. Consent to audio record; filed under "research participant identity LP". Interview took place in room at a branch library close to participant's home address. The room was private.

Val: So, Lucy, could you tell me about your relationship with Milo?

Lucy: It was amazing when we first met. He swept me off my feet; I felt so special.

Val: How long have you and Milo been married?

Lucy: Two years. We met at uni, but he only stayed there for two terms before he left and started a business. So, I've known him about four years.

We got married in my last year of uni.

Val: What about you? Tell me about yourself.

Lucy: Mum and Dad divorced when I was little. It was a bit brutal. Dad couldn't forgive Mum for wanting an independent life. It went through court after court. They wouldn't even talk to each other. When me and my brother saw Dad, he would pull up outside of the house and then Mum would put us outside of the door and shut it behind us.

(Reflexive comment on transcribing recording. Did she shudder at that point? Or did I shudder as I imagined what that might have been like for a small child?)

Lucy: Then later there was the court order that meant he wasn't meant to know where we lived, so we met him somewhere, I think it was a church hall or something, and there was a bunch of ladies who watched us. Dad wasn't allowed to take us out of the hall. I remember it being so hot in the summer and knowing Dad was angry. I always felt I had done something wrong.

Val: And now, looking back, what do you think?

Lucy: I'd love to talk to Mum about it, and my brother, but it just feels like something that can't be done. I don't even know where Dad is now. When I was doing A levels, he just suddenly stopped showing up. No messages, texts – nothing.

(Reflexive comment made when transcribing recording. Did a tear form in her eye at this point? She looked burdened to me, and I felt a bit "sullied". Need to explore that more. Did she see what happened? Could she see the behaviour as domestic abuse or was she shielding herself from that kind of possible knowledge?)

Lucy: When Milo and I married, I thought now we could have children and it would be so different for my children to what it was like for me. Milo and I would never do that to our children.

Val: But?

Lucy: Now he says he doesn't want children. He has a good job. He is well paid. He says I don't need to work because he can provide for me.

Val: What did you train to do?

Lucy: Work with children in early years settings. I loved it.

(I remember her face lit up when she talked about this.)

Val: And now?

Lucy: I do the admin for Milo. That's how I got to see your letter, and I thought I would get in touch. I thought maybe if I talked to you, I'd understand him more.

Val: How do you mean?

Lucy: I don't know anything about him. He is different now. He said I didn't have to work but if I don't help out in the business, he calls me a sponger. I see my friends starting their families or choosing to develop their careers, and I think I should be so grateful for my life. I have everything I want: I can go to the gym when I want, I can indulge in my hobbies, I even have help in keeping the house up to scratch. But it's all about keeping things just how Milo wants it. I am starting to feel like my mother.

(Lucy started crying at this point. I don't think she realised about feeling like her mother until she said it. Truth dawning is painful. Milo sounded like a bully. Note made when transcribing the recording: I see I changed the subject quickly but unhelpfully.)

Val: How is Mel?

Lucy: Mel?

Val: His mum?

Lucy: He doesn't talk about family. He said he was adopted. He's mentioned a Tony and Sarah? I think he said they were his parents.

(I couldn't remember if Sarah and Tony were his birth parents. I was aware of growing alarm that Lucy didn't know about Mel.)

Val: Lucy, are you all right? Do you feel safe with Milo?

(I don't know what prompted me to say that, but Lucy really started crying at this point.)

Lucy: I think I might be pregnant. I didn't mean to be; he's going to be furious. I really don't want to be like my mother.

Val: Are you telling me that you don't feel safe with Milo?

Lucy: No. Not really. I don't know. It's probably my fault. I just do things badly.

Val wrote in her diary:

I am worried about Lucy. It sounds to me as if Milo could be coercively controlling, but I don't think Lucy is at the point of realising that yet. I feel guilty. I never thought someone else would open a letter addressed to Milo. I felt as though she came hoping I had some kind of magic solution for her. I did give her the name of a therapist and encouraged her to go, but the look on her face made me think she wouldn't be able to. I think I got myself into an unethical position that was neither research nor therapy.

Then, tucked into Val's research diary, was a newspaper cutting dated four weeks after the date of Lucy's visit and the transcribed conversation.

Young entrepreneur killed in road traffic accident. Pregnant wife in hospital.

Milo Peters (24) owner of Peter's Carpet Warehouse was killed when his BMW left the road and hit a tree. No other vehicles were involved. Lucy Peters (24) was cut free and taken to hospital. A hospital spokesperson said there was no risk to either Mrs Peters or her unborn child, but she would be kept in hospital for observation. Police are appealing for anyone with information about the black BMW yesterday evening.

Val sat down when she read the headline in the paper. It seemed such a strange coincidence that she should have seen Lucy so recently. She carefully tore around the newspaper article and slipped it inside the pages of her research journal. Milo was part of her tribe; part of the process that led to her being the person and the therapist she was proud of. She couldn't just let his death go unmarked.

Val contacted Mel. It was so easy to trace her contact details with the internet and newspaper reports. Mel was keen to talk and they met in a coffee shop. Mel suggested a place she knew that was quiet, which was at the back of the local auction house. Val found her way through the odd assortment of other people's no longer wanted items, some valuable, some junk, and found Mel waiting for her. Mel seemed oddly stiff in her posture as they sipped their coffee and made small talk to catch up.

It was a while before Val felt comfortable to ask, "What happened?" She had the road accident in mind; Mel's thoughts were clearly elsewhere.

"It was fine until he was fourteen. Then it was as if he just started to fade away from us. From being able to let me see what was going on so I could help him find expression for stuff, he just pulled back and pulled back. I was wild with terror and asked for help, but people said it was 'just adolescence' and that as an independent person he had to want to be helped. I just knew it wouldn't happen. I just knew it was more than that."

Val could hear and see the hot angry tears.

"No one would listen, and we lost him. He was never 'bad enough' to be excluded from school. He worked OK and got exams. He went to uni, but once he had gone there, that was it. He stopped coming home. He dropped out really quickly. I do admire him for what he did. He got a job at the carpet place and worked his way up really quickly, but I don't think I've had a proper conversation with him since he was fifteen. I feel like I have been bereaved, but no one sees what I have to mourn. It's not just him killing himself. The biggest hurt was when social workers seemed to suggest it was my poor parenting that had driven him to this. I gave up my chance to have another child because your work with us showed me that he would need extra help and care throughout his childhood. I loved him, but I lost him even before he died."

"Killed himself?" Val picked up.

"Oh, that slipped out. I don't think he would have done it deliberately, but he was so reckless at times." Mel's voice was monotone, her delivery unwavering in speed, her eyes fixed just underneath the level of Val's gaze.

"What about Simon?" Val asked.

"We just slipped apart too. I worked so hard trying to support Milo that

I didn't notice how unhappy he was. Then he had an affair with someone at work. They are still together. I can't say I blame him. It was all pretty joyless with Milo."

Val spent two hours with Mel and left profoundly sad. Mel seemed to have lost all her warmth and energy. She kept circling back in her thinking to the unfairness of the way she and Milo had been treated when she'd asked for help. She blamed this for his death. Her anger had found nowhere to be received, heard or acted upon, so anger had sunk into bitter depression.

Val attended Milo's funeral. Later, she stood at his graveside. She placed down a single rose for him.

I loved you as much as I could, she thought. *I am so sorry it wasn't enough.*

She recalled how close she had been to burning out when she was working with Milo and Joe. She remembered sitting with Brenda after she'd made such a mess of a session with Milo and then lost it with her when she thought Brenda was suggesting she was using the work with children to meet her own needs. She remembered understanding in that moment how she and the boys all shared the deepest wound – not being held by their mother. That understanding had emerged for her when she found the courage to go back to Brenda. There, she had been able to face what felt like her deepest shame: she had needs, too, that she wanted her mother to meet, but her mother couldn't.

Joe had had the best deal, despite experiencing the worst events. Something had been kept alive for him. A belief in the goodness of humankind that had a power and desire to care about others. Val had discovered it through her work with children and in her relationship with Brenda – a belief in the goodness of humankind and her own goodness as a kind human. She discovered that, yes, she learnt about herself through her work with the children, but not in a way that diminished the children. They learnt together – her committing to her own self-knowing so she could help them find themselves. She cared, professionally, with commitment and skill. She grieved for Milo and his suffering, and her life would continue to be fruitful because he was worth living for.

She heard the voice of Brenda in her thoughts: "So, Val, what's next?"

Val bent down and picked up a handful of soil from the grave.

"I will love the Milo inside myself and try to show people that he did what was necessary to keep himself together in the best way he possibly could."

Val walked down the hill from the graveyard. Her car was parked near to a children's play area. As she came down towards the car park, she saw a little girl run out of the playground.

"No, Niks!" she heard someone shout. She assumed it was the little girl's mum. "No ducks today. We need to go home now."

The little girl spun around and put her hands on her hips. She looked about four, maybe five. Val was too far away to see her eyes, but she assumed they sparkled because to her it looked like the whole of the girl sparkled with life.

"No!" the little girl shouted.

Val smiled. She was beautiful! Val couldn't say what was beautiful because of the distance, but something about her — her liveliness, her energy, her wiry intensity — it kind of reminded her…

"Joe, can you sort her out. Sammy's pooed, and I need to change his nappy."

Val looked closely; she couldn't see. It couldn't be, could it?

A young man stepped out towards the little girl. It was! Val was about to call out when she saw him pull something from his pocket.

"Niks, I bet you can't pop this bubble with your elbow. I know you've got the best bubble-popping elbow in the world, but the wind might blow the bubble away."

She could see the girl hesitate, caught between the desire of the duck and the desire for her dad. Unperturbed, Joe was blowing a bubble.

He knows she'll come! Val thought.

The bubble grew, and grew and grew, until it left the bubble wand.

"Quick, Nickie! Get that sharp elbow here!"

But she wasn't quite fast enough; the bubble drifted too high.

"Daddy, I missed it!"

"No, you didn't!" Joe picked his daughter up and tossed her into the air, the bubble bursting when her head hit it. Firmly, Joe caught her on the way down and put her carefully on the ground.

"Silly Daddy! That was my head!" the little girl said.

"Oh dear! I'd better blow some more, then," Joe said as he bent down and kissed the top of her head. "So, this is a head. Where is an elbow?"

She showed him, and he kissed her elbow too before blowing more bubbles. They disappeared back into the playground.

Val took the path the other way to get back to her car. She opened the door and sat in it. It was hot, so she opened the window while thinking. She could see them all now through the play area fence. Val was pleased she hadn't called out, not wanting to intrude on the family.

Joe was getting the little girl to help put away what must have been their picnic things. He put sandwich boxes on her head and counted her down: one, two, three, drop! The boxes landed in the bag he was holding.

Val couldn't see the baby on the ground, nor could she hear the mum, but she could see from the way she was moving and the looks on her face that she was enjoying the nappy change. Then, yes! She could see two little feet being held gently in two grown-up hands and two grown-up cheeks being puffed out to be popped with those two little feet. She couldn't hear the laugh of the mum or the chuckle of the child except what she could see with her eyes and feel in her heart. Joe must have taught them that!

"Daddy, can we do blanket swing!" The little girl was shouting.

She saw Joe look towards the woman. She guessed, hoped, it was Shell. They exchanged an unspoken parent moment, and then Joe said, "Of course. Just let Mummy put Sammy in the pushchair."

Gently, Shell strapped the baby in as Nickie lay down on the picnic rug. This clearly wasn't a new thing for her.

Val pulled her seat belt around her and secured it.

Joe and Shell picked up the blanket.

"Twinkle, twinkle..."

Val started her engine and backed out of the parking space. The song continued in her head: "Great big stars. Oh, what lovely people you are."